BREAKING
NEWS

BRIAN MOONEY & BARRY SIMPSON

BREAKING NEWS

HOW THE WHEELS
CAME OFF AT REUTERS

CAPSTONE

First published 2003 by
Capstone Publishing Ltd (a Wiley Company)
The Atrium
Southern Gate
Chichester
West Sussex PO19 8SQ
England
www.wileyeurope.com

CIP catalogue records for this book are available from the British Library and
the US Library of Congress

ISBN 1-84112-545-8

Typeset by Forewords, 109 Oxford Road, Cowley, Oxford

Printed and bound by T.J. International Ltd, Padstow, Cornwall

This book is printed on acid-free paper responsibly manufactured from
sustainable forestry in which at least two trees are planted for each one used
for paper production.

Substantial discounts on bulk quantities of Capstone Books are available
to corporations, professional associations and other organizations.
For details contact John Wiley & Sons: tel. (+44) 1243 770441,
fax (+44) 1243 770517, email corporatedevelopment@wiley.co.uk

Contents

Style note

Reuters house style is not to use an apostrophe when the company's name is used in the possessive sense, a convention we have followed throughout

1

A Poisoned Chalice

I n one armchair sits Jeremy Paxman, one of Britain's
best-known, often feared television interviewers. Facing him
is a relaxed and smiling Sir Peter Job, newly knighted chief
executive of Reuters, one of the most famous companies in the
world.

The pair is flanked by giant TV screens, cameramen training
lenses on the stage on which they sit. Below them in the cavern-
ous ballroom of London's Grosvenor House Hotel is an
expectant audience of 1,200 current and former staff of the
global news and information giant, now celebrating its 150th
anniversary.

The occasion, in July 2001, also marks the retirement of Job
who, after ten years at the helm, is handing over to Tom Glocer,
a former mergers and acquisitions lawyer and the first American
and first non-journalist to head the company.

Reuters is riding the crest of a wave – three decades of virtually uninterrupted growth. But, although profits are running at

record highs, cracks are beginning to show. The share price, driven up to all-time highs in the dotcom craze, is 40% below its peak, and only the previous day Reuters has announced more than 1,000 redundancies.

Nobody really seems to care. Reuters has had its ups and downs with the markets before and has always ridden out the downturns. Job is not going to let this latest blip spoil the party and responds to Paxman's questions in his customary self-congratulatory tone.

"Would you recognize a bus if you saw one, Sir Peter?"

Paxman gives Job an easy ride – this is, after all, a PR gig, not *Newsnight* – ribbing him gently about his journalistic background and his comment that, now aged sixty, he qualifies for a bus pass. "Would you recognize a bus if you saw one, Sir Peter?" he asks the multimillionaire captain of industry.

Less than two years later, Reuters is trading at a loss and the share price has crashed to less than 10% of its peak. Its market capitalization has slumped from £23bn in March 2000 to £1.4bn, far outstripping the decline in the FTSE-100 index over the same period.

Job has said he regarded his principal achievement as "exiting smoothly with the business in good shape and a seamless hand-over to a successor I respect". But he has handed Glocer what seems to have been a poisoned chalice and serious questions are now being asked about his ten-year stewardship of Reuters – once one of Britain's flagship companies, now vulnerable to an unwelcome takeover.

Did Job and his fellow directors fail to renew Reuters, fail to prepare for a vicious downturn in the markets? And if Reuters really was in such 'good shape' when Job handed over, what turned it so rapidly into the shape of a pear? Few inside the company will deny that something – apart from the sheer force of a savage bear market – went badly wrong.

The reality is that there were two Reuters in the 1990s. Viewed from outside, Reuters ruled the world with a powerful brand that meant trust, impartiality and reliability. It was a glamour stock. Its screens were bolted to the desks of the world's major banks, financial institutions and corporate treasury departments, and its news, photos and video sold to newspapers and broadcasters around the world. Here was a powerful technology firm with leading-edge networking, delivering data and connectivity to the global trading room, combined with the world's biggest news organization, each side bursting with university educated, technically savvy, capable and motivated staff. With some 20,000 staff running 230 multimedia news and financial services offices in 150 countries around the globe, few companies were better poised to exploit the golden opportunities of the Internet Age.

But inside Reuters things looked decidedly different. It had developed a product no one was using, and it had been sucked into a string of potentially damaging law suits and investigated by the FBI. Preoccupation with shareholder value was sapping its risk-taking entrepreneurial energy and Reuters had failed first to notice and then to head off the challenge of a new competitor, Bloomberg. As the Internet Age arrived, Reuters found itself without any clear strategy, uncertain whether it was a technology or information company or a bit of both, and unable to exploit its obvious advantages. And while senior managers indulged in high living, major divisions of the company were torn apart by a destructive succession battle.

This is a story of missed opportunities, of failure to renew, of a company that gets carried away with technology without knowing where it will lead. It begins with a businessman and would-be banker from Germany who became a successful journalist, and ends with a former mergers and acquisitions lawyer from New York taking over a beleaguered business from a bunch of journalists who thought they had become bankers.

PIGEON POST

Reuters made virtually no money for its first 120 years. It had survived that long thanks to a mix of entrepreneurial risk-taking and careful thrift, a few subsidies and subventions here and there, and a hard-earned and jealously guarded reputation for reliability. The launch in 1973 of a screen-based financial information service, Monitor Money Rates, changed all that almost overnight. The ex-journalists running the company expected to sell a few dozen Monitor screens around the world. When the Monitor network was shut down twenty-six years later, having been superseded by generations of even more successful products, there were over 500,000 Reuters users worldwide. Reuters had pioneered a global electronic marketplace. Commercial success does not come much bigger.

This giant of the media and financial world had risen from humble origins. Its founder, Paul Julius Reuter, was born in 1816 in Kassel in central Germany to a prominent Jewish family.

After an unsuccessful venture into publishing a news-sheet in Paris, he returned to Germany in 1849 and spotted the opportunity that was to ensure his place in history.

Telegraph had spread rapidly throughout Europe and the United States in the 1840s, though not until the mid-1860s would the continents be linked. The French government's telegraph line to Brussels remained closed to the public, however, and there was also a significant gap in the network between Brussels and Aachen on Germany's western border, which meant news despatches and commercial information such as stock prices had to be carried by train between these cities, for onward dissemination by telegraph.

In 1850 Reuter acquired carrier pigeons to carry news despatches the 76 miles between Brussels and Aachen, covering the distance in around two hours, less than half the time taken by the train. From Aachen these could be telegraphed to Berlin for newspaper and financial clients prepared to pay a premium for the faster delivery Reuter offered, with the same service offered in the opposite direction. The premium for speed was a principle that would underlie the news and information empire that would make his name known around the world.

The advantage offered by Reuter's 'pigeon post' was short lived. The gap in the telegraph network was closed in April 1851, barely a year after his birds had first taken wing. But undaunted, and now convinced of the growth potential for telegraphed news, Reuter moved to London, itself about to be linked to Europe for the first time with the laying of a Dover–Calais submarine cable.

The Industrial Revolution and the growth of the British

Empire had made London the financial capital of the world and Reuter set up a service to provide opening and closing prices from the London and Paris stock exchanges to clients in both capitals. The service was expanded to provide information on the all-important international grain markets. European news-papers took political news from London from Reuters, though British newspapers resisted taking its news from Europe until 1858.

By the 1860s Reuter's agents were reporting from the far-thest reaches of the Empire, as well as America where Reuter reached an agreement with the Associated Press in 1862 to ensure good coverage of the Civil War. News from the other side of the Atlantic still came by mail steamer, and Reuter had agents at the main ports in mainland Britain and Ireland to dis-tribute news and market prices as soon as the steamers arrived. One notable coup, in 1865, was a two-hour 'newsbeat' on the assassination of Abraham Lincoln more than ten days earlier.

'Follow the Cable' became Reuter's maxim. The steady spread of telegraph to the four corners of the world enabled Reuter to expand newsgathering, and also to widen the spread of newspapers and financial institutions able to subscribe to his services. Alexandria became the first office outside Europe in 1865, followed by Bombay the following year, Valparaiso in 1874 and Cape Town in 1876. Reuter retired as head of the agency in 1878, handing over to his son Herbert, but continued to serve on the board. He had been created a baron by the Duke of Saxe-Coburg-Gotha in 1871 and his baronetcy was con-firmed in Britain twenty years later by Queen Victoria.

Baron Paul Julius de Reuter died in Nice in 1899 at the age

of eighty-three. A year later Reuters scored one of its greatest-ever scoops, on the relief of British troops besieged in Mafeking during the Boer War. Its Pretoria correspondent learned of the breakthrough from the Boers and travelled to the Mozambique frontier to avoid their censors and get the story out. His telegram reached London the day after the relieving column broke through, triggering wild celebrations throughout Britain. Queen Victoria asked to see the original telegram, and it was another two days before the story was confirmed through military channels.

In 1925 the Press Association (PA), owned by the provincial press, bought a majority stake in Reuters, taking 100% control five years later. In 1939, just weeks before the outbreak of World War Two, Reuters and the PA moved to 85 Fleet Street, their new joint headquarters designed by Sir Edwin Lutyens, which remains Reuters Head Office to this day.

Another change in ownership came in 1941, when the national newspapers bought 50% of Reuters from the PA. An important part of the new arrangement was the Reuters Trust agreement, in which the PA and the nationals' umbrella group, the Newspaper Publishers Association (NPA), agreed to regard their shareholdings "as in the nature of a trust rather than as an investment", pledging to ensure Reuters "integrity, independence and freedom from bias" in return for cheaper access to its news. The Australian and New Zealand Press Associations took small shareholdings after the war.

Reuters finances nevertheless remained far from secure. Revenues grew steadily, reaching £2.4m in 1960, but profits were miniscule with the financial services, now grouped under the name of Comtelburo, subsidizing the costly and unprofitable general news service. Waiting in the wings however, were three men who were to transform Reuters fortunes over the next two decades.

TAKEOFF

The first of these was Gerald Long, who became general manager in 1963. Recruited from Cambridge at the age of twenty-five, he was fluent in French and German, a bluff Yorkshireman of humble origins but formidable intellect. He had risen rapidly through the ranks, becoming chief representative for Germany in 1956 after spells as a correspondent in Paris and Ankara, then assistant general manager for Europe in 1960. A tall, heavily-built man with close-cropped hair, bristling moustache and penetrating gaze, he could be an intimidating figure.

The second was Michael Nelson, head of Comtelburo since 1962. He had joined ten years earlier as a trainee journalist, a graduate of Magdalen College, Oxford, serving in London and the Far East before moving into management in London. In marked contrast to Long, he was a quiet-spoken, thoughtful man, though possessed of considerable toughness, vision and decisiveness.

The third key figure was an Australian, Glen Renfrew. On graduating from Sydney University he had done what many young Australians do – toured Europe. Arriving in London in 1952, he had walked into 85 Fleet Street and asked for a job, and was given an editorial position in Comtelburo. Relaxed and easy-going with a broad Australian accent, he developed a strong interest in technology, which was later to stand him in good stead. Assigned first to South Africa, then Singapore, he became head of a new Comtelburo computer division in 1964.

"Reuters could easily have disappeared in the 1960s."

Long recognized that drastic change was needed to ensure Reuters long-term future and the survival of the news service, its *raison d'être*. Had the nettle not been grasped, according to Nelson, "Reuters could easily have disappeared in the 1960s."

Here was a small British company owned by newspapermen who were not going to invest heavily in its future, faced as they were by the newly-arrived threat to their advertising revenues from commercial television. Unlike its main US competitor, AP, it had no strong domestic market base – just 58 newspapers compared with AP's 1,700 – and no government subsidy like Agence France Presse and other European state-owned news agencies.

The breakthrough came in 1964, when Reuters entered into a joint venture with a New Jersey company, Ultronic Systems. Ultronic produced a rudimentary desk-top computer terminal with a three-digit display and keyboard known as Stockmaster, which provided access to US stock market and other exchange information. The agreement gave Reuters exclusive rights to Stockmaster outside North America for ten years, and Reuters doubled its transatlantic communications capacity to introduce the service to Europe. Ultronic provided all the equipment for the venture, removing much of the financial risk for Reuters.

The system was soon highly profitable and Reuters added a

master computer in London to make European stock and commodity exchange prices available. By the end of the decade it had installed over 1,000 Stockmasters in Europe, and the service was extended to Tokyo, Hong Kong, Australia and South Africa.

In 1970 Ultronic introduced a new screen-based terminal with a 72-digit display, providing a much wider range of data. By 1974 Stockmaster and Videomaster had contributed £4m in profits to Reuters coffers, and at minimal risk, Ultronic having provided most of the capital and equipment.

INTO THE STRATOSPHERE

The new decade brought another opportunity that would transform Reuters. In 1971 the Bretton Woods Agreement, formulated in 1944 to ensure post-war economic stability, was dismantled and with it went its central platform of fixed exchange rates.

"This was going to revolutionize the markets and we'd better see how we could exploit it."

"We decided that we had better look at the implications of this for Reuters," Nelson recalls. "This was going to revolutionize the markets and we'd better see how we could exploit it."

André Villeneuve was another Oxford graduate, who had joined as a trainee journalist in 1967 and moved swiftly into management. Nelson sent him to Switzerland to talk to major banks. The problem was that, unlike stock and commodity markets, there was no trading floor for foreign exchange, spot and forward rates being set by telephone and telex between banks, brokers and their customers.

Villeneuve drew up a proposal for a system to display banks' exchange rates for major currencies on Reuters screens. The idea had an element of cheek to it. On one side of the service were contributing banks, who would insert rates into their own 'pages' on the system. Recipients would pay Reuters solely to view the data, but contributors would also be charged for the privilege of inserting their own data.

The proposal went to Nelson early in 1972, and he took just days to weigh the risks and rewards before putting a formal plan to Long. He in turn put it to the board, few of whom, being newspapermen, had much idea of what it was all about.

The costs were modest by today's standards – a loan facility of £800,000 was arranged though only £200,000 was drawn in 1973 when the service was launched. But Reuters was a poor company, so the risk was significant. Nevertheless, the board acquiesced.

Expectations for the service were also modest. Only a few dozen subscribers were anticipated, and the computer system behind it was designed to accommodate just a couple of hundred. When the Reuter Monitor foreign exchange market quotation system was launched in mid-1973, there were just fifteen contributors and the same number of recipients, all banks. London brokers feared the greater transparency the system brought to the market would threaten their business.

In October 1973 war broke out between Israel and its Arab neighbours, and the Arab oil producers imposed an embargo on supplies to punish the West for its support for Israel. Oil prices more than quadrupled and financial markets were thrown into turmoil. The increased volatility of the foreign exchange markets might have been expected to provide a huge boost for Monitor, but it was almost its undoing.

"Markets were going wild because of the oil shock, and there was a danger that the Reuters Monitor would fail."

"Markets were going wild because of the oil shock, and there was a danger that the Reuters Monitor would fail, because people were too busy to use a new instrument," Nelson recalls. "The paradox was that the very conditions we had hoped to exploit were there, but they came a little bit too early."

The problem was that contributors had to insert rates manually, a slow and cumbersome process which was later automated. "It was a tremendous *tour de force* by André to persuade people to use Monitor despite the fact that, because of the turbulence of the markets, they were too busy to put their rates in," Nelson adds.

Within a year, Monitor had outstripped all expectations with 250 subscribers to the 'green screen' – bright green characters on a black background – in the UK and Europe, a figure which had grown to 1,000 by late 1976. Money News Retrieval, which enabled clients to view news on the Monitor screen rather than teleprinter, was launched in 1975. Market-moving newsflashes appeared at the bottom of the screen regardless of what page a user was viewing.

The breakthrough that would place Reuters at the centre of the foreign exchange markets for a generation was the FXFX page. This multi-currency display was created by automatically transferring rates from major contributors to a single page, enabling users to see every key change in the market in one place instead of trawling through individual banks' pages. FXFX became the window of the foreign exchange market, and came to symbolize Reuters unique success.

Reuters had stumbled upon a way of making money twice out of the same piece of information, with contributors paying to insert their rates and users paying to view them – and in so doing had created the first global electronic marketplace. FXFX entered the language of the dealing room but also insinuated itself into Reuters as the benchmark by which all acquisitions and subsequent business proposals would be judged. In the eyes of one consultant, the company developed an 'FX fixation'.

More data and news was added to the system – bonds, equities and US government securities. Reuters was virtually unrivalled in news and information for the plethora of spot and futures markets for commodities and in 1981 launched a highly successful service for the oil markets which, in the heyday of OPEC, had a major influence on most financial markets.

Such was the success of Monitor that Reuters spent the next decade struggling to keep pace with demand and to expand the systems behind it to handle the huge flow of data. Within ten years of its launch Monitor had generated £100m and Reuters turnover had leaped to £242m from £17.5m – an annual growth rate of 30%. Profits soared to £55m from just over £1m in 1973, a compound growth of almost 50% a year.

Monitor was not entirely a lucky accident – Long, Nelson and their colleagues had identified an opportunity in the collapse of Bretton Woods and moved to exploit it. But they could not have anticipated the explosive growth of foreign exchange and money market trading in the years following its launch, and never in their wildest dreams could they have imagined the success Monitor would enjoy, the millions of pounds of profits it would generate. They had gone panning for gold nuggets and stumbled across Eldorado.

FLOATING ALOFT

With much of the credit for Monitor's success down to him, Nelson became general manager in 1976. Renfrew had moved to New York in 1971 to head Reuters North America, and the two men were appointed joint deputies to Long, now managing director. By 1981, Long was restless after eighteen years at the helm. "He was clearly bored with Reuters, and there wasn't much more he could have done for it," says Michael Reupke, then editor-in-chief.

Long had become close to Rupert Murdoch who, as chief executive of News International, owner of *The Times*, *Sunday Times*, *Sun* and *News of the World*, was a director of Reuters. The recently acquired *Times* was floundering, and the two had frequently discussed how it could be shaken up.

"Long came into my office one day and said to me: 'Murdoch has just offered me the managing directorship of *The Times*'," Nelson recalls. Asked how he had responded, Long replied: "It took me all of two minutes to say 'yes'." He hadn't even asked how much he would be paid.

Murdoch wanted someone who was acceptable to the British establishment, and who could have fitted the bill better than the managing director of Reuters? But the move was not a success. "His problem was he knew nothing about newspapers," Nelson observes, "A very different matter from running a news agency." He lasted just a few years. The move also, ultimately, meant he lost out on a fortune.

To the great surprise of many, it was Renfrew who succeeded Long. Nelson had been the driving force behind the growth of the previous twenty years, but Renfrew, with his enthusiasm for technology, was felt to have more ambition for the future.

Another major change was in the wind. Reuters profits had quadrupled in 1981 and more than doubled the following year, and it began to dawn on the proprietors that their shares in what was once a small 'family news agency' were now potentially worth millions. A campaign began for Reuters to go public, to unlock this new-found wealth.

"I felt a flotation for Reuters was a bad idea, although I did not fight it very hard."

The debate was divisive. Chief among those pressing for an early float was Lord Matthews, a Trustee of Reuters and chairman of Fleet Holdings, which owned the *Express* group. Less convinced was another Trustee, Associated Newspapers chairman Lord Rothermere, whose *Daily Mail* was the *Express*'s biggest rival. Murdoch himself told the authors in a recent letter: "I felt a flotation for Reuters was a bad idea, although I did not fight it very hard."

There was some speculation he might eventually seek control of Reuters himself but, according to one director at the time, Murdoch was "on the side of the angels" seeking to ensure Reuters' integrity was protected, rather than siding with the handful of proprietors who were apparently solely concerned with how much cash they could extract.

Renfrew had been sceptical, seeing no need to tap to the stock market for capital, although he, Nelson and company secretary Nigel Judah were now shareholders, having been given a new class of non-voting shares in 1981. Renfrew changed his mind when the US company Telerate, Reuters biggest competitor in the financial markets, launched a highly successful flotation. Not all within Reuters were convinced, though, the journalists in particular fearing the company's independence would be under threat.

The run-up to the flotation was a long and complicated business, centring on a new Trust agreement and a share structure compatible with the Trust principles as well as attractive to both proprietors and potential investors.

The eventual solution was a 'Founder's Share', a single share controlled by an expanded board of Trustees able to outvote the entire issued share capital in the event of any threat to the Trust principles. There would also be two classes of voting shares, 'A' shares retained by the proprietors and 'B' shares offered to the public, but with the A shares having four times the voting weight of the B shares. This was not liked by City institutions and many boycotted the flotation. As a result, the share issue raised less than earlier projections, which had put Reuters total value in excess of £1bn.

In April 1984 a new company, Reuters Holdings, was set up and three new directors brought in – Christopher Hogg, then chairman of Courtaulds, Walter Wriston, head of the US banking giant Citicorp, and Volvo chairman Pehr Gyllenhammar. Reuters became a public company on 4 June through a flotation on the London and New York exchanges of some 25% of the equity – 106.8m shares at £1.96 a share, valuing the company at around £800m.

Reuters itself raised £50m in new capital and Renfrew, Nelson and Judah became millionaires. Dozens of managers with share options found themselves wealthy overnight, but every member of staff was given the right to buy a modest allocation of shares at a favourable price. Gerald Long got nothing.

The windfall for the newspapers, totalling around £150m, transformed Fleet Street. The City boom which followed financial market deregulation had sharply pushed up Fleet Street property values and this, coupled with the Reuters millions, enabled the proprietors to invest in new offices and print works embracing the latest technology, sweeping away the infamous restrictive practices of the print unions.

Murdoch's move in 1986 to 'Fortress Wapping', his secretly built new plant east of Tower Bridge, is the best-known example, with daily TV news footage and newspaper accounts of staff running the gauntlet of enraged print workers. But others followed suit, moving to new plants on the south bank of the Thames and elsewhere and, within a few years, not a single national newspaper remained in Fleet Street.

2

Masters of the Universe

Jonny Fitzgerald had always been something of a showman. Both parents were actors – father Walter counted Squire Trelawney in the film of *Treasure Island* among his credits – and, with his natural gregariousness, Fitzgerald was a born salesman. In 1979 he found himself trying to sell something that didn't exist.

Reuters had considered the possibility of a transactional element to Monitor, enabling banks actually to deal via the network, at the time of its launch, but realized that a more robust technical infrastructure and greater development effort would be needed, so the project was kept on the back burner. Nelson, though, saw that there was nothing to stop a competitor such as Telerate launching such a system, which would have threatened the survival of Monitor, now vital to Reuters.

"They would see what it was supposed to do and the idea was to get them to say: 'Yes, if you produce this, we will take it.'"

19

Reuters worked closely with potential customers to develop a dealing system, and a decision was taken that it would be launched only if a critical mass of banks would agree to sign up in advance. Fitzgerald recalls having to persuade London treasury managers simply on the basis of a slide show. "They would see what it was supposed to do and the idea was to get them to say: 'Yes, if you produce this, we will take it.'"

The development cost some £8m – more than double Reuters pre-tax profits in 1980 – and launch was postponed several times as rigorous testing continued to ensure the system could meet stringent reliability targets. When the Reuters Dealing Service finally went live in February 1981, it had 145 clients in nine countries in the US, UK and Western Europe.

Reuters had ceased to be just a provider of information, and was now a medium through which currencies could be traded, an integral part of the foreign exchange and money markets. Over the next year the Dealing Service was extended to Hong Kong, Singapore and the Middle East, but progress remained slow.

John Lowe, also a sales executive at the time, later to become managing director for the UK and Ireland, says the service lost money for the first two years and brought Reuters 'perilously close' to insolvency. It was a 'brave decision' by Nelson to stick with it, he adds.

Nelson is more modest. "I think the brave decision was doing it at all," he says. "Once you'd spent the money on getting it going and overcoming the tremendous problems there were, it would have been foolish to have stopped it."

Within three years the system was handling tens of

thousands of calls between banks daily. Reuters now had two major cash cows and started milking them with near-monopoly pricing power, country managers often charging whatever they could get from their local markets. Pre-tax profits in 1984 were nearly £75m compared with less than £4m five years earlier. And it wasn't going to stop there.

BUYING BUSINESS

The second half of the 1980s saw Reuters embark on a wave of acquisitions, driven largely by Renfrew who firmly believed that rapid growth was the only way forward for Reuters.

The first major acquisition was Rich Inc., a Chicago-based manufacturer of video switching systems, which Reuters bought in 1985 for a little under $60m. Rich took Reuters into the highly lucrative trading rooms systems market. The years since the collapse of Bretton Woods and deregulation of banking and financial markets had seen explosive growth of trading in foreign exchange, money, equities and commodities, as well as the wide range of options and other derivative instruments related to them. Markets had also become increasingly inter-related and, as a consequence, dealing rooms had changed beyond recognition. Vast trading floors at the major institutions now often housed hundreds of dealers, over a thousand at some of the global financial giants.

Providing individual terminals to potentially hundreds of dealers had become a cumbersome and expensive process, and IT managers were looking for better-integrated solutions. Customers were also clamouring for discounts at sites where they had dozens if not hundreds of Reuters screens, a concession Reuters was initially reluctant to give way on. Both demands could, however, be met with the help of Rich. Its technology enabled Reuters to provide feeds to hubs installed at its major client sites, to which individual desks and dealers could then be connected, achieving big economies of scale and, at the same time, giving customers a cheaper 'multi-keystation' deal.

Rich's earliest systems had been solely analogue, switching just screen displays between traders' desks, but it soon became evident that the way ahead would be digital. In 1987 a digital switching system known as Triarch was introduced, enabling individual bits of data to be assembled into custom-made displays. Reuters was ahead of the game. It realized it could capture the systems business and started integrating datafeeds from competitors such as Telerate into its trading room systems. This was the beginning of a Reuters love affair with technology which would gradually shift the client relationship from end-user to IT department and would, over time, have a damaging impact on the business.

But by the end of the 1980s, revenue from rental or outright sale of trading room systems was over £160m a year, more than 16% of total revenues which had topped £1bn for the first time in 1988, with pre-tax profits of over £200m.

Another spectacularly successful acquisition was Instinet, a US equities trading service bought in 1986 for $100m. This allowed buyers and sellers such as fund managers to trade block of shares 'off market' and anonymously. Heinrich Wenzel, Director of Global Accounts until 2001, describes its purchase as "one of the smartest things the company did in the 80s."

Fitzgerald, who headed Instinet sales and marketing in the UK, describes how it worked. "One guy may be rebalancing his books and just happens to want to get rid of say, 10 million IBM. Not that there's anything wrong with IBM, but he's just rebalancing because he's long in computer stocks. IBM's trading at $110–112, but if he puts all that stock on the market the bid will probably go down to $105. Then, maybe somebody the other side of the world says 'actually I need some IBM because I'm rebalancing,' so they meet in the middle (via Instinet) and trade at the middle of the spread and both sides are happy. It's not reported to the market until the trade's done, so the fact that 10m shares have changed hands doesn't affect the price."

Reuters had no idea what a goldmine it was taking on. Instinet took time to gain market acceptance, and Renfrew had to battle with his fellow executive directors to keep it going. But as it started to take off, new Instinet offices were established in London, major European centres such as Frankfurt, Zurich and Paris, and Hong Kong and Tokyo, to trade non-US equities. It became a big money-spinner, handling tens of billions of dollars a year in securities transactions. One senior Instinet executive estimated it contributed around $1bn to Reuters profits in the 1990s. Instinet revenues grew steadily, reaching over $1.4bn in 2000, though rising costs meant profits levelled off around the $140m mark towards the millennium.

Not all acquisitions were so successful. Reuters had also in the mid-1980s acquired a position-keeping system from Hovland Business Systems, allowing foreign exchange traders to keep an automated record of their transactions and outstanding positions through a touch-pad 'tablet' on their desks.

23

One top sales executive, himself a former foreign exchange dealer, recalls seeing a demonstration. He watched with interest as the means of recording spot and forward deals was outlined, then asked how it dealt with money market deposits – the interest rates on which were a key determinant of forward rates – only to be met by blank stares. Despite lacking this vital element, Reuters launched it anyway.

"There were massive holes in it, huge great holes, from the very beginning. And you had to pretend there weren't, because somebody at the top had made the decision to go ahead with it."

"They just didn't understand," he says. "There were massive holes in it, huge great holes, from the very beginning. And you had to pretend there weren't, because somebody at the top had made the decision to go ahead with it."

Another acquisition was the improbably named Schwartzatron, a sophisticated system for evaluating complex strategies in the US options markets, bought in the late 1980s for $7m. The machine was the brainchild of Steve Schwartz, a huge, shambling bear of a man, a former options trader and a mathematical genius. With a long, straggling mane of hair fringing a bald pate, Schwartz roamed his Chicago offices in a moth-eaten pullover, baggy cords and sandals on bare feet. Invited to address the Reuters board, he had to be dragged to the shops to buy a suit, shirt and tie. Efforts to integrate Reuters data with the system proved fruitless, and the new acquisition quietly faded into oblivion.

Nevertheless, the shopping spree continued at a furious

pace, broadening the product range rapidly. Other acquisitions in the Renfrew era included IP Sharp, a Toronto-based database of market data, and Finsbury Data, a London news database which formed the foundation for Reuters diversification into historical news retrieval.

Reuters paused for breath after Renfrew's retirement, then launched into another frenzied wave of acquisitions after Peter Job took over. On the media front, it bought 18% of ITN, news provider for independent television in the UK, and AdValue Media in the US, a system to allow advertisers to buy TV airtime on-line.

In 1994 it bought stakes in Teknekron, a California developer of dealing room systems software which later became TIBCO, and Citicorp's financial information system Quotron, the culmination of twenty-five acquisitions in the space of twelve months. Teknekron, a $125m acquisition, in many ways competed with Triarch – somewhat confusing for clients – but was bought partly to head off its possible acquisition by Bloomberg.

Reuters also bought VAMP, a British provider of healthcare information systems to doctors, and Reality Technologies in the US, an online provider of personal finance information. By the end of the decade Reuters had some 250 subsidiaries, both acquisitions and its own operating and other companies.

"We are planting acorns . . . We will have to see if they turn into oaks."

"We are planting acorns," Job told an interviewer in 1994. "We will have to see if they turn into oaks."

Crucially, though, Reuters never went for the big one, the acquisition that would represent a major diversification away from its core dependency on the upper-tier financial markets and, in particular, on money and foreign exchange. Reuters seemed to pin its hopes on the little acorns, but not often were they given the time, money or management backing to grow. The risk-taking and the entrepreneurial guts that took Reuters into developing Monitor and Dealing were rarely put behind them.

Indeed, many acquisitions disappeared virtually without trace, including a myriad of small, local products running on technical platforms incompatible with Reuters own systems. Sometimes, too, the company's left hand did not know what the right was doing. In the late 1990s it made major investments in two competing electronic order routing systems for market trades – GL and Liberty – in effect buying the same technology twice from outside the company while, at the same time developing similar technology *inside* at Effix.

Reuters never seemed able to define and stick to an acquisitions strategy. Initially it was a story of careful building on and adding to the core business, both on the trading and technology side. Some, like Rich, Teknekron and Instinet, were hugely successful. Later there was a phase of buying outside the core business in the hopes of striking another FX-like goldmine. This led Reuters to acquire businesses in health and advertising and move into such diverse fields as shipping, air cargo and insurance.

"Reuters has trashed more subsidiaries than you can shake a stick at."

Had some of these been followed through with committed management they might well have turned into goldmines – especially if they had been harnessed to the Internet. But many Reuters investments and new ventures appeared haphazard, were poorly integrated into the group, if at all, and were badly supported. Many acquisitions and new ventures foundered, although Reuters is by no means unique in this. But, as one former senior marketing executive says: "Reuters has trashed more subsidiaries than you can shake a stick at."

MATCHMAKING

Reuters had first considered automated trade matching as part of Dealing in the late 1970s, but development of the initial conversational dealing system took priority. The baton was picked up in the 1980s by Reuters development team at Hauppauge on Long Island and work began in 1986 to develop a prototype system.

The initial idea had been to come up with a system to bring together buyers and sellers of US government securities, which had become a vast market of global importance on the back of years of US government budget deficits, financed to a large extent by Japanese investors.

"If you guys produce this system, I will personally see to it that you never do any more business in New York."

But major US brokers could see a large part of their market disappearing if Reuters were to successfully launch such as system, just as Monitor and Dealing had reduced the role of money brokers. Fitzgerald, by now a senior sales executive in New York, was given the task of sounding out the top Wall Street firms. He recalls the head of one telling him: "If you guys produce this system, I will personally see to it that you never do any more business in New York," a threat echoed by others along The Street.

There was a similar reaction from the Chicago commodity futures exchanges when Reuters touted the idea of developing matching for those hugely important global markets. Reuters, the Chicago Mercantile Exchange and Chicago Board of Trade joined together to launch Globex, a matching system for Chicago-traded commodity futures outside the markets' normal trading hours in 1992, but Reuters pulled out of the venture within a couple of years.

That left the old standby, the foreign exchange and money markets. In 1989 Reuters had launched Dealing 2000, a Windows-based terminal for the original conversational dealing service. The first Microsoft Windows information terminal, the Advanced Reuter Terminal, or ART, had been launched three years earlier, combining Monitor data with news, graphics and eventually spreadsheet capabilities.

Matching technology was by now well understood, although one potential problem to be overcome was that of so-called 'broken trades' where, through a technical fault or telecoms failure, one party might think the deal was done while the other didn't. This could have left Reuters, as effectively the broker, carrying potentially significant risk for any financial losses arising from broken trades, so a two-way confirmation system was developed, delaying the launch for a year.

When the new system, Dealing 2000-2, was launched in April 1992, the banks were impressed and some of the leading foreign exchange players raised the possibility of a joint venture with Reuters to operate it. Partnerships, however, were not part of the ethos of Reuters, which liked to do things its own way.

The banks were unhappy about the prospect of an effective Reuters monopoly in matching and, indeed, had been researching their own system for a couple of years. The delay in the Reuters launch resulting from the broken trades issue had given them time to catch up, and in 1993 a group of major banks launched a rival system, EBS, which, according to one senior Reuters marketing executive "completely ate Reuters lunch".

In 1990 Reuters hired Ros Wilton from Drexel Burnham Lambert (DBL), and she soon took over transactions products, including Dealing. It was one of the first times the company – now generating over a billion pounds a year from the financial markets – had bought in top-level expertise from the markets.

"This project's going to cost at least five Wiltons."

Wilton's reputedly huge salary became the subject of widespread gossip, even entering the Reuters argot as a measure of money: "This project's going to cost at least five Wiltons." Wilton dismissed talk of her salary as petty jealousy but found little in common with most of her new colleagues. The feeling was mutual, few having a kind word to say about her.

Perhaps because of the mutual animosity, there were few significant further developments in transactional products. Instinet continued to grow, but the Dealing cash cow was starting to run dry, even though Wilton had been tasked with expanding the transactions business.

With bank mergers and the approach of the euro, which was going to sharply reduce the number of traded currencies, Dealing client numbers peaked at 25,000 in 1997, taking a small dip the following year. Wilton briefly joined EXE, the executive committee of top managers that ran Reuters, in 1998 but was gone a year later. Client numbers continued to slip, and by 2002 Dealing revenue had dropped to £278m, 35% below its 1998 level. Client numbers were down to 18,000 by 2003.

EBS, meanwhile, in which major partners include Citigroup, ABN Amro, UBS and Credit Suisse, was going from strength to strength, by 2003 handling over 40% of the $200bn-plus daily spot foreign exchange transaction volume, and dominant in yen, dollar and euro trading.

In May 2003 EBS and Bloomberg announced they were teaming up to offer the EBS Trader conversational dealing service over Bloomberg terminals, in a direct attack on Reuters already struggling foreign exchange and Dealing businesses. Bloomberg's head of foreign exchange Kevin Foley characterized the partnership as "the most important thing we have done in foreign exchange" while EBS's chief executive Jack Jeffrey said the goal was to win 10,000 users within three years – inevitably at Reuters expense.

"This has taken us 20 years to build up and we are still number one," Reuters managing director for treasury services Julie Holland responded. "We are the innovators. They are playing catch-up."

The irony that it was Reuters rejection of a joint venture

with the banks which prompted the formation of EBS passed largely unnoticed.

In July 2003, though, Reuters fought back with a law suit in New York accusing Bloomberg of infringing patents on the matching technology in its Dealing systems.

NEW NETWORK

By the late 1970s the original Monitor network was groaning under the strains of its explosive growth. There were 200,000 screens worldwide and the old network and Quotation Retrieval System (QRS) could barely cope. The Integrated Data Network (IDN), brainchild of a visionary engineer, Richard Willis, rose in its place. For better and for worse, it would power Reuters financial information business into the 21st century.

Monitor and QRS were based on retrieval technology. The user entered a code for the required data or news on the keyboard and the terminal's controller retrieved it from a central system. Although it normally took a couple of seconds, retrieval times could stretch during periods of heavy market activity.

IDN, one of Reuters biggest technical triumphs, was based on an entirely different principle, a proprietary high-capacity global network broadcasting the entire array of information gathered by Reuters between three main data centres in London, New York and Hong Kong. These in turn rebroadcast the data by satellite to smaller regional data centres and clients' own IDN terminals – new colour screens offering considerably more flexible displays than the old green Monitor screens – and subsequently onto the Windows-based Reuters Terminals (RT).

One of the key figures in drawing up the marketing specifications for the system was Herbie Skeete, who also wrote the product specifications for the first services delivered over IDN. Caribbean-born, a gregarious six-footer with an infectious sense of humour, he is one of the very few of Reuters 'old guard' to have survived, coming largely unscathed through countless management culls over twenty years.

"They can't fire Herbie, he's black," colleagues say, tongue in cheek. His survival is more likely down to his unquestioned expertise in the technicalities and intricacies of exchange data, on which he is an acknowledged authority, both within Reuters and the wider financial community. The *Handbook of World Stock, Derivative and Commodity Exchanges*, which Skeete edits as a profitable sideline, has for years been a standard industry reference work on stock, derivative and commodity markets.

IDN's first phase went live in October 1986 and the first IDN subscriber service, Securities 2000, incorporating the new US equities feed, was launched the next year, followed by products for the money, commodities and bonds markets. IDN set new global standards for information products, giving Reuters a five-year lead over competitors, and remains to this day the foundation of its real-time information systems.

IDN's strengths were remarkable but it needed constant re-engineering to keep it current. Built to carry 100 updates a second, its capacity is now in excess of 20,000. IDN propelled Reuters through its boom years but, as Internet technologies offered simpler and cheaper solutions and the tide began to turn in the financial markets, it left the company weighed down with a network on which it was hard to achieve economies of scale.

IDN's broadcast architecture is configured in such a way that, by default, it distributes all data everywhere. Some bits of data circle the globe three or four times before reaching a client's terminal.

"Getting the right balance of which data was going to be sent where and at what price should have been tackled much earlier."

"It's a bit like an airline," says former Technical Director Martin Davids. "You build up an infrastructure for a given level of business and, when that business falls away, it's hard to quickly get to the level that it should be. All data everywhere as a business model was obviously not going to work forever. Getting the right balance of which data was going to be sent where and at what price should have been tackled much earlier."

THE END OF AN ERA

At the end of the 1960s Reuters annual turnover was less than £9m. By the end of the 1980s it was a shade under £1.2bn, while pre-tax profits had soared from a mere £200,000 to close to £300m.

It had been a period of remarkable growth, fostered by three key men – Long, Renfrew and Nelson. Reuters had been transformed from a widely respected but financially vulnerable news agency into a global news and market data giant and pioneer of a worldwide information revolution.

Mistakes had been made. Some acquisitions would not easily bear the scrutiny of hindsight and others had not been nurtured. A degree of arrogance had also crept in. Reuters appeared to have become seduced by such innovations as Monitor, news retrieval and Dealing and allowed itself to believe it could lead the markets into new technologies, whether they wanted them or not. Technology, in part because of the sheer complexity of Reuters now global business, was starting to take over.

But the arrogance and creeping dominance of technology were scarcely visible. What stood out was the success of Monitor and Dealing, and the two key acquisitions, Rich and Instinet. If mistakes had been made, surely future generations of Reuters leaders would learn from them?

Three rising stars had moved into the upper echelons of Reuters management – Peter Job, David Ure and André Villeneuve. All three had joined from Oxford University in the 1960s as trainee journalists; they had grown with Reuters and assumed senior management roles in the early 1980s, before being appointed to the board in 1988.

All three, so the story ran in Editorial, had become managers in the first place only because they did not make the grade as journalists. As a journalist in the 1960s, the theory went, if you made a mistake it could have serious consequences and damage Reuters all-important editorial reputation. As a manager, there was nothing terribly serious you could screw up.

Villeneuve stayed too short a time in editorial for any judgement to be made. Ure, one former senior executive recalls, "never quite won his spurs", perhaps explaining an apparent enduring ambivalence towards editorial. Former editor-in-chief Michael Reupke, though, springs to Job's defence: "Peter was a good journalist. Not a great one; he wasn't one of those correspondents who would have made headlines everywhere, but he was a good journalist."

Villeneuve had distinguished himself through his role in the development of Monitor and later Dealing. In 1981 he had become manager of Reuters Europe, taking over North America two years later when Renfrew finally released his hold on his former fiefdom.

Ure had also been actively involved in the development of Dealing. European marketing manager under Villeneuve, he moved up a slot when the latter transferred to New York, taking over the geographical area responsible for more than half the company's turnover and profits.

A lugubrious Scot, Ure was generally viewed as the most cerebral of the three, much given to pensive scratching of his nether regions in meetings, whilst pondering some seemingly intractable problem or even when talking with visitors. One former press officer recalls taking a female American journalist to see Ure. She watched in astonishment as he unconsciously scratched his way through the interview. "Does he always do that?" she asked later. "Do what?" the press officer replied innocently.

Job was the brashest and most obviously ambitious of the three, and had the widest geographical experience. In 1978 he had become managing director for Asia (including Australia and New Zealand), achieving a more than tenfold increase in its revenues by the end of the 1980s.

In 1989 Michael Nelson announced his retirement from Reuters. He had been disappointed eight years earlier when

Renfrew had succeeded Long, but few would dispute that he had been one of the most influential figures in Reuters history, and a principal architect of its transformation over the previous two decades.

"There was a willingness to consider new ideas, as long as they were produced in a very disciplined manner, properly thought through and the research had been done."

"There was a willingness to consider new ideas, as long as they were produced in a very disciplined manner, properly thought through and the research had been done," a former executive committee member recalls. "And then they got to Nelson, and decisions were taken."

Another senior colleague, though often irked by Nelson's punctiliousness, commented: "He said 'no' to a damned sight more stupid ideas than he did good ones."

Nelson was a good judge of people, as well as ideas, and also widely seen as the guardian of the 'family values' of the old Reuters through an era of rapid change and growing commercial complexity. He once instructed a regional manager to reinstate a veteran correspondent who had been fired for supposedly having a drink problem and embarrassing Reuters through ill-judged remarks to a Latin American government minister while 'in his cups' at a company reception.

"This man has served Reuters well for many years, often in extremely dangerous circumstances," Nelson told the offending manager. "If he has a drink problem, we don't fire him, we bring him back to London and help him through it."

Renfrew was to follow Nelson into retirement in 1991. His

contribution had been immense, both his hard-headed approach to growth through acquisition as well as organic expansion, and his commitment to new technologies. His decision to get IDR to produce bespoke equipment for Reuters was also something of a triumph, saving the company millions of dollars, as was his conversion to PC technology. This came at one legendary meeting when a young technical manager from Kentucky, Buford Smith, convinced him that Windows was the way ahead. In an almost Pauline instant, the IDR manufacturing phase was over and the Reuters Terminal was born. Reuters led the way into open systems and became Intel's first corporate customer. Reuters, on balance in the 1980s, seemed to make all the right strategic technical decisions – adopting digital data-feeds, IDN, satellite broadcast and the RT.

"He had a lot of vision, a lot of drive. He was frequently wrong, but there was a sort of entrepreneurial nature to Renfrew that energized the whole company."

"He had ambition and vision," a former member of executive committee says. Another senior colleague believes the Renfrew era was the last time Reuters had an identifiable strategy. "He had a lot of vision, a lot of drive. He was frequently wrong, but there was a sort of entrepreneurial nature to Renfrew that energized the whole company."

Throughout that astonishing period of dynamism and growth, a culture of quirkiness and eccentricity had been tolerated, even fostered within the company, as a stimulus to creativity and invention. It was, in the words of one former senior executive, "an extraordinary culture which drove us all to work so hard, which attracted such talented people, which made us feel so proud to be Reuters employees."

Nowhere was that more true than in Editorial, where the sense of being part of a great enterprise dedicated to the highest traditions of journalism, but also being witness to and bearing responsibility for accurately and impartially recording events both great and small for posterity, were palpable.

That sense of uniqueness flowing from Editorial permeated the entire company, and it was not just hard work, the executive recalls. "I don't think most people could understand just what fun it was to work for Reuters in its heyday."

This extraordinary culture, he adds, was also a key competitive asset, "a factor in explaining why Reuters made so much money and dominated so many markets when Telerate, Bridge, Quotron and others all failed."

THE MAN WHO RODE A TIGER

As Renfrew approached retirement the battle to succeed him narrowed down to a two-horse race, Job versus Ure. Nelson preferred either Ure or Villeneuve, whom he had hired and trained. But Villeneuve had made little mark on North America since taking over from Renfrew, managing it largely on a care-and-maintenance basis. To have changed anything, one senior manager commented, "would have been an implied criticism of Renfrew". Another executive who worked closely with him says "Villeneuve boxed beneath his weight." Few saw him as a serious contender.

Ure reflected Nelson's management style and personality, the carefully considered, more studied approach. Although he had only managed a second-class degree at Oxford, he was generally seen as a first-class brain, an incisive thinker. But he was, by common agreement, not the world's greatest communicator. A dour personality, he was frequently compared to Eeyore, the gloom-laden donkey in *Winnie the Pooh*. He had what colleagues called a 'poor user interface' and would perhaps not have made, many felt, a good public face for Reuters.

The bluff, hard-driving Renfrew backed Job, again more in keeping with his own style and personality. He considered Job more hands-on, more aggressive, a go-getter, and an opportunist. As deputy business manager in South America in 1973, he had tied up a communications deal with Augusto Pinochet only days after the General had overthrown Salvador Allende's elected government in one of Latin America's bloodiest coups.

With a remarkable grasp of detail, Job was never slow to speak his mind on any topic, not just Reuters but almost anything under the sun. Although his syntax was frequently tortured and his metaphors mixed, he was ever the communicator.

Neither Job nor Ure had a markets background and neither in the end ever got really close to the markets.

"Despite his self image of a 'man of the market', Peter did not have a good appreciation of the market beyond bun-fights with dealers in Hong Kong restaurants," according to Bruce Allen, an Australian and Job's marketing director in Asia. "He visited many clients but it was more to do with projecting his image than understanding what they wanted," he adds. "David

Ure, on the other hand made little pretence of being a man of the market and avoided client contact as much as possible."

Job became chief executive in 1991. His management of Asia had been an unqualified success, albeit during an explosive period of economic growth throughout the region. In the eyes of one marketing executive, Job in Asia "rode a tiger that had some room to run".

His skill had been to milk the Monitor and Dealing cash cows for all they were worth. He had also been nimble and inventive. He pioneered small dish satellite delivery for news and financial services, a technology that would enable Reuters to sweep into newly-liberated Eastern Europe after the downfall of communism, and he started some innovative local services. But on the whole he had been able to run Asia on the back of things produced elsewhere and there had been little actual development in Reuters Asia beyond bolting on local and regional variants to these core products. The value of his one significant acquisition – a graphics solution called ESL – was questioned elsewhere in the company. Job's ability to handle global development and technology issues was yet to be fully tested.

He had, though, been an inspirational leader. He worked hard to understand the detail of his country managers' businesses and to get to know and motivate and reward their staff. In return, he earned their loyalty and energy. One striking example was a sales conference held in a top hotel in Singapore in 1988 for well over a hundred sales executives from as far afield as Japan, New Zealand and Morocco, as well as sales and marketing managers.

At the end of a busy few days of new product demonstrations and sales training, the managers staged an elaborate cabaret to entertain their staff at the closing dinner. Reuterizing the lyrics of well-known songs, backed by professional musicians and with a rising star of marketing, Krishna Biltoo, face whited-out *à la Cabaret*'s Joel Grey, as compère, sales managers donned garish drag to seduce a supposed top banker to the strains of *Big Spender*. Another strutted his stuff in an astonishing Mick Jagger impersonation while the grand finale was a rendering of *Life is a Cabaret* by a top-hatted, tail-suited marketing manager:

> *What good is working for Villeneuve or Ure, Europe or RNA?*
> *Asia's the place to be, old chum, come selling for PJ . . .*

Job joined the soloist on stage for an encore and, though hopelessly out of tune, earned rapturous applause from the audience. A consultant 'sales guru', brought out from London to conduct a series of seminars, said he had never in his long career seen such *esprit de corps* in any company.

Despite Ure's disappointment, Hogg, who had become chairman in 1985, kept the triumvirate together, Ure assuming global responsibility for marketing and technical policy while Villeneuve came back from New York to head the company's geographical units. It was perhaps Hogg's first major mistake. Their rivalry for the top slot aside, Job and Ure had never been close and the new setup did nothing to change that.

"You have to wonder whether they communicated at all."

"You have to wonder whether they communicated at all," one former senior executive says. "They met at board meetings and executive committee meetings, but it was a pretty uneasy setup. And you've got the chairman in the corner congratulating himself on keeping them together. Maybe the fact that he kept them together wasn't a success at all."

How serious a problem could that apparent lack of management synergy be? The next few years would show. For the time being, all eyes were on the bottom line. Since the flotation seven years earlier the share price had more than quadrupled, as had annual profits, now running at £320m. Reuters employed more than 10,000 staff in 180 offices worldwide, and was undisputed market leader in news and information.

3

Battling Bloomberg

Michael Rubens Bloomberg, founder of Bloomberg LP, is now Mayor of New York City with an official residence on Upper East Side just off Central Park and ornate offices in City Hall in Lower Manhattan. Bloomberg has status, and huge wealth with which he has pursued public office and a lavish lifestyle. *Forbes* magazine estimates his fortune at $4.8bn, making him the twenty-ninth richest man in America and sixty-third in the world.

David Mulhall, a former Reuters marketing executive, is a neurological development consultant, treating dyspraxia and related disorders from modest premises in a side street in Battersea in south London. Mulhall is neither rich nor famous.

Mulhall's and Bloomberg's stories converge over bonds.

Bloomberg used to trade bonds for the US brokerage house Salomon Brothers. They sacked him and he took his $10m redundancy cheque and built Bloomberg LP, arguably the most successful player today in the financial services markets.

Mulhall had been a research analyst studying bonds and other financial markets with Lloyds Bank, and in portfolio management with Joseph Sebag before joining Reuters in 1975.

Bloomberg spent several years after leaving Salomon methodically building up a database of market trades from a closed user group at Merrill Lynch, then launched a service which combined this resource with clever, easy-to-use analytics. In contrast to Reuters, which had propelled Monitor and Dealing into the market from the outside, Bloomberg had started out with a partnership with one of the biggest global names in the world of finance. Bloomberg's company prospered and grew slowly but steadily through the 1980s, but few executives at Reuters saw him as anything more than a brash, self-praising niche player, a minor irritant about whom the company's most senior British managers would often crack jokes.

"I told them over and over again that you've got to watch this guy Bloomberg and they would do everything they could to throw orange peel at me."

"I told them over and over again that you've got to watch this guy Bloomberg and they would do everything they could to throw orange peel at me," says a former American executive. "They would respond by saying it was a closed system and too expensive, and that he was just an arrogant trader."

The real-time markets for money, equities and news were what made the world spin at Reuters – and the only major threat then was from Telerate, which Reuters systematically and successfully overwhelmed. Nevertheless, at the dawn of the 1980s it had been pre-eminent in coverage of bond market prices.

Mulhall was one of a small band inside Reuters who saw Bloomberg coming, even before the launch of the Bloomberg terminal. He had been heavily involved in setting up Reuters International Bond Service in the mid-1970s and, returning to head office from a stint in Hong Kong, he was in 1983 put in charge of the bonds department in central marketing. Reuters offering to the bonds traders at the time was little more than a few indicative prices on Monitor, on which they could not execute deals. Bloomberg's, on the other hand, would provide a broad range of prices direct from market traders and, most important of all, offer an historical cache of these prices and clever analytic tools that were easy to use.

Mulhall realized Reuters needed to build a database of prices and set about developing a system that would analyse and compare instruments. By 1989 he had designed a product that would have incorporated all short-term instruments, especially US government bonds, and he had built a computer simulation to demonstrate just how an analytics product would function.

"I'd specified a product which I think would have knocked Bloomberg for six. It would have allowed interrogation by country, by year, by quality or rating, with direct links to news directly affecting each market," he says.

"Money was put in the budget, but it was used for other things. I think it was seen as a bit of a joke."

Mulhall argued that Reuters had to wake up to the threat to Bloomberg. "Money was put in the budget, but it was used for other things. I think it was seen as a bit of a joke, with the bond market of little relevance compared with money markets and equities. Sadly, it never happened."

Ure, more interested in equities markets, did not even look at Mulhall's computer simulation. "All sorts of schemes that are not fully cooked come up from marketing departments," Ure now says. "I don't particularly remember the Mulhall contribution."

Mulhall was made redundant three months later, 'out of the blue', he says. But, while his plans were not followed through, he left behind an awareness that Reuters had no strength in historical or stored data. His experiences mark the beginning of an extraordinary relationship between the two vendors in which Reuters view of Bloomberg developed from dismissing him as a niche player into regarding him with outright fear. The one constant is that Reuters never got it right. Over the next ten years it was to make a series of attempts to catch up with, overtake and in marketing terms 'kill' Bloomberg – all of which were to come to grief.

No one who worked for Reuters during those years can recall any customer asking it to create an alternative to Bloomberg. The call to arms was an internally driven obsession and, in the end, Reuters never managed to think far enough out of the box to move on to other more creative ways of consolidating its market position rather than simply trying to copycat and outsmart its competitor.

Reuters and Bloomberg were at heart two fundamentally different concepts. Reuters was a real-time system which pumped out market rates and prices then threw them away. Bloomberg was a database that collected prices and price history and saved them for future reference. This was the fault line on which Reuters repeated attempts to compete foundered, and it was always going to be easier for Bloomberg to add real-time data than for Reuters to build a database that would complement its real-time information. Reuters failure to come to terms with this fundamental difference was already apparent in the way Mulhall's proposal was brushed aside.

David Brocklehurst, one of Mulhall's colleagues in marketing at the time, recalls discussions about his proposals 'going round in circles'.

"The key issue was that we would need a very different architecture and network to deliver the product," he says. "We would need a big central computer which was on-line to thousands of terminals around the world. The computer would need a huge central database and search and calculation engine and this, of course, did not fit with the distributed architecture and real-time refreshing set up of IDN and Monitor.

"David Ure had a blind spot for the architecture and could not get his mind round the need for yet another network and the cost of a large central computing system."

Ure, who maintains he was "very alive to the Bloomberg threat from the late 1980s", at that stage had overall responsibility for historical data and was also hotly engaged in the front-line of the battle to succeed Renfrew.

"Renfrew at the time had set very strict and very demanding targets for real-time data and historical data which were nothing to do with Fixed Income," a senior technical manager recalls. "I think Ure got his brain around it all. He just did not like the cost and the risks at a career turning point."

Before ever thinking in terms of competing head on with Bloomberg, Reuters had a succession of inconclusive meetings with him. Brocklehurst recalls one key encounter in New York in late 1986.

"My brief, which I had planned and discussed with David Ure, was to try to secure some sort of marketing deal with Bloomberg. We had already determined that it was an excellent fixed-income product with a good database and analytics and a very solid reputation in the US market."

"Our approach was to ask if he would be interested in Reuters marketing his product – outside the USA and around the world. Bloomberg considered the proposition for all of about five seconds."

"He showed us the product and his operation in New York. He had not yet started marketing the product outside the USA. Our approach was to ask if he would be interested in Reuters marketing his product – outside the USA and around the world. He considered the proposition for all of about five seconds. His response was that he was flattered, that he had a lot of respect for Reuters, but that he felt his business would get tied up with too much bureaucracy and that he liked to do his own thing. So 'thanks, but no thanks'. The meeting, guided tour and lunch took several hours. He took delight in demonstrating the Bloomberg product personally and was obviously very proud of his creation."

There were other meetings with Bloomberg, the most significant with Ure, also in New York. This time Bloomberg and Ure discussed the possibility of Reuters providing its news to

Bloomberg in exchange for Bloomberg allowing Reuters to carry its service on Reuters Triarch. But Ure said he would not give Reuters news to a competitor and nothing came of the discussions. Years later he was still justifying his decision.

"Bloomberg would just have exploited our news to his advantage."

"Bloomberg would just have exploited our news to his advantage," he subsequently told a group of managers.

The result was that Michael Bloomberg, now with 10,000 screens installed around the world, took the battle to Reuters home ground. The one advantage Reuters still had over him, at least in the fixed-income market, was news. So in 1990 Bloomberg launched his own news service. It was a momentous decision and, although for many years Bloomberg news was considered less comprehensive and authoritative than Reuters, it quickly developed a character of its own, and a following.

HIRED KILLER

At about the same time, Reuters took another tack. The company, still under Renfrew, had entered into several strategic partnerships and made a number of timely acquisitions. Some, such as Instinet, the share-dealing system, were to prove immensely profitable. A lot of the deals were brokered by Renfrew and Ure.

In 1989 they reached an agreement with Stephen Levkoff in the first serious attempt to outflank Bloomberg, and the first clear sign that the company had woken up to the threat. The relationship was to prove a costly mistake for both parties. Reuters initially approached Levkoff, a senior vice-president at Smith Barney, to develop a product to compete in Bloomberg's home market. He joined forces with Reuters as a consultant working through his own company, Capital Markets Decisions (CMD), based in Stamford, Connecticut.

A Reuters product, known as Decision 2000 and nicknamed by Reuters managers the "Bloomberg Killer", emerged from this partnership in 1991. The product was basically a failure and by 1993 relations had soured to the point of a law suit, although a settlement was eventually reached out of court in December 1993.

"The deal remains confidential but I was not happy," says Levkoff. "What I got out of it was probably 20% of what it was worth."

Neither Levkoff nor the Reuters people who worked with him for almost four years now have a good word to say for each other. Piecing together the story more than a decade later leads to at least one inescapable conclusion – that the partnership was a cul-de-sac for both Reuters and Levkoff.

Levkoff has no doubt that he came out badly. He portrays Reuters as company run by a bunch of journalists who had struck lucky with foreign exchange but knew next to nothing about financial markets.

"They were great on news and great on forex," he says. "With forex they were in the right place at the right time. The company was run mainly by former journalists and they did not know all that much about the financial markets. They certainly never understood fixed income."

"They entered loose contracts and they rattled the sword when it suited them."

"Our Decision 2000 data was aimed at the fixed-income market. They wanted my data. We went through a variety of situations when every time you turned round Reuters wanted to change the contract. They entered loose contracts and they rattled the sword when it suited them."

Key technical issues blighted the relationship from the start. Reuters had recently bought a database, IP Sharp in Toronto, and invested in a company called ESL which produced graphical displays and some rudimentary analysis of data. Reuters aimed to leverage off both to create a product with Levkoff. The problem is that Levkoff – rightly or wrongly – quickly concluded that both IP Sharp and ESL were not up to the job.

"It was a pretty bad database."

"Reuters was into information display. They had bought a database, IP Sharp in Toronto, but I refused to use data from there. It had a 50% error rate. Their data was either incorrect or just not there at all. It was especially lacking on bonds data. It was a pretty bad database."

He had worse to say about ESL, a Sydney-based company run by David Vanrenen, a South African entrepreneur who had also developed a rudimentary bonds analytical service, Giltnet. Levkoff was brusquely dismissive of ESL's software and told Reuters he could build a better package – he wanted a bigger slice of the action. He was not alone in dismissing ESL. Several Reuters technical managers in North America had reached similar conclusions about the product and one had found and negotiated a deal from an alternative source – Townsend, a Chicago-based company.

"Townsend had a package that worked on Windows," one of the Reuters technical managers involved recalls. "We negotiated a great deal with them which would have given us the product and source code for $2m."

But Windows at that time was far from a dominant 'must-have' system and Asian marketing managers decided to do a revenue-split deal with ESL because they had a 'windowing like' application and because of their track record in delivering a product to Telerate – Giltnet. Townsend was also seen as a less attractive route because it wanted up-front cash and was not willing to share the risk.

Vanrenen himself puts the criticism of ESL down to the fact that Reuters in the US was automatically dismissive of anything not developed there – the 'not invented here' syndrome prevalent throughout much of Reuters, which was run in jealously guarded territorial fiefdoms. ESL, he says, "had a history of delivering good and groundbreaking products."

"Reuters Asia was pretty naïve. But Windows in the late 1980s was far from a great product and nobody knew where it would go."

With hindsight one of the marketing managers involved says, "Reuters Asia was pretty naïve. But Windows in the late 1980s was far from a great product and nobody knew where it would go."

"The result is that Reuters throughout much of the 1990s never had a really good graphics display," the former technical manager says. "They ended up with a Mickey Mouse package that cost millions of dollars and never really delivered."

"They ended up with a Mickey Mouse package that cost millions of dollars and never really delivered."

Another executive involved in the deal looks back at it this way: "There was a big debate between Reuters North America and Reuters Asia on which was the better to use globally at Reuters. Merit was clearly not the only factor on either side. It was political. Also, ESL had more of a proven track record with products launched in Australia and Japan and with Telerate in the US. Townsend had no record at the time. Having said that, was Townsend a more talented better group? Probably. At the time it was hard to judge. In retrospect, time has shown it's pretty easy to make that call."

"Reuters has lacked technical visionaries and still does."

"One clear theme at Reuters is that when presented with two or more possible paths in technology or architecture, Reuters has chosen poorly – but through no great fault or negligence of anyone. The correct path is never obvious, especially in times of real structural shifts. But Reuters has lacked technical visionaries and still does."

With the full support of Job, both before and after he became chief executive, Reuters poured more than $20m into ESL before it was finally closed down in 2002. Although mostly incidental to what was going on in Levkoff's CMD, the ESL story came home to roost at Stamford in one very crucial aspect. This was in Hubert Holmes, a soft-spoken American southerner with an MBA from Columbia whom Job had recruited as an acquisitions executive in Asia in 1986. Job had seen other parts of Reuters making strategic acquisitions and it no doubt crossed his mind that pulling off some good deals in Asia would enhance his standing back in London.

Holmes was involved in the integration of Vanrenen's company into Reuters and eventually moved from Asia to London as managing director of ESL, which was initially based at Vanrenen's house in Walton Street in the heart of London's fashionable Knightsbridge.

By then Job had become chief executive and Holmes got a call that would lead him to Stamford and a critical role in two dramas that would unfold there. Job phoned to tell him that Reuters had a problem in Stamford and the problem was Levkoff. Holmes was tasked with sorting it out and, while he continued to have direct access to Job, he now officially reported to one of the coming men in central marketing, Krishna Biltoo. By his own admission, Holmes was no great expert in fixed income – he was assigned to CMD as a 'relationship manager'.

A Reuters executive who watched the relationship at close quarters said Holmes at first threw himself enthusiastically into the task of trying to make two massively different cultures work together. But he found Levkoff difficult to get on with and, worse, he was not persuaded by his product which was launched as Decision 2000 on a joint marketing and royalty basis.

"Decision 2000 was way too ambitious . . . It ended up being another technology issue. It looked like crap."

54

"Decision 2000 was way too ambitious," the executive recalls. "It tried to deliver across all fixed-income assets globally and really what it could do was a number of fixed-income asset types. It ended up being another technology issue. It looked like crap; I've got to admit that. It had a green screen in a world that was moving on to Windows. It's too simplistic to say it was crap. The product had some potential and customers thought so too, but it was never executed well enough to deliver. That data side was ridiculous."

Sales and marketing executives in the field were less polite about it. A London marketing executive said Levkoff delivered rubbish and became uncontrollable.

"The original business deal was based on him producing a product that would sell globally and for which he would be paid," he recalls. "But basically he promised everything and delivered nothing. We employed a sales force of more than 100 around the world but sales never came. It took a day to work out that the product did not work.

"The joke in London was that it took two people to demo the product. One to do the demo and the other to distract the customer with jokes when it broke down."

"The joke in London was that it took two people to demo the product. One to do the demo and the other to distract the customer with jokes when it broke down."

Sales complained and the tone of the relationship changed dramatically, with vitriolic messages winging their way between Levkoff and critics in both the US and Europe, many couched in highly colourful language.

Levkoff maintains Reuters claimed the product did not work as part of a strategy to cut him out. "As for the suggestions that Decision 2000 didn't work properly, that was a rumour started by Reuters to discredit me. Without equivocation, it worked, and Reuters supported the product for years because some of their top clients had no other source of multi-currency portfolio analytics."

Reuters Bloomberg Killer was "not an overwhelmingly successful product."

Whatever the verdict, by 1993 it was clear Decision 2000 was not living up to expectations inside Reuters. In September, Ure, in masterful understatement, acknowledged to a meeting of analysts in New York that Reuters Bloomberg Killer was "not an overwhelmingly successful product".

Heinrich Wenzel says Decision 2000 was 'deeply misguided'. "In money terms it might not have cost a lot, but it cost a bomb in reputational terms."

As the relationship slid out of control, a final confrontation took place over ownership of the data Levkoff had created for the product. Levkoff thought it was his, Reuters believed it owned the copyright and at some stage started to recreate the database so that it could cut free altogether from Levkoff.

"Levkoff became more and more vitriolic at meetings and more and more demanding, and started to hold Reuters hostage to the data that he was creating. We considered that data was a Reuters asset. It was our intellectual property. Levkoff thought we were trying to create a competitive product, so there was fundamental disagreement on who owns what, who gets what," a former senior executive involved in Decision 2000 says.

"We started a project, fearing that the data would be held hostage or that he would turn it off or do other things that would be detrimental to Reuters reputation and its customers, and we recreated the database. We wanted a structured transition and we told Steve this. He fought back behind the scenes but it was contractual, we had the right. So he grudgingly came along. We also put together a plan to take over and be able to manage the operations of Decision 2000 ourselves if all of a sudden Steve should shut it down. People were hired to do that, which Steve did not know about."

Reuters began talking to Levkoff about buying him out but the negotiations broke down – on at least one occasion Levkoff walked out of a meeting saying he had a tennis date. On 19 October Reuters finally pulled the plug and turned off his data connections. Levkoff sued and the case was only resolved after protracted wrangling. He had originally asked for $50m for his company and in the end settled for under $10m.

The Levkoff case was the first major test under fire for Simon Yencken, a hard-nosed lawyer hired by Job from Australia to head up a new corporate legal department in London.

"Levkoff never expected Reuters to play hardball," says the Reuters executive involved. "He thought he could just bully Reuters out of lots of money – a strategy that had worked up to then."

Yencken became a man to fear, sacking almost every lawyer at Head Office and setting about creating a new legal empire, which at its height had eighty lawyers worldwide. Reuters, as former US investor relations manager Mike Reilly puts it, was at that stage 'lawyering up'. One of Yencken's first hires in New York was a young Wall Street M&A specialist, Tom Glocer, destined to become the first American to run Reuters.

"We wasted three years."

Barry Drayson, a forex and derivatives broker, and one of a new breed of highly paid market experts recruited in 1990, looked back at the Levkoff experience as being one of Reuters most costly mistakes. "We wasted three years," he says.

TRYING TIMES

Drayson, who left Reuters in 1999, unwittingly led it into another hugely disruptive law suit. This one involved the major US brokerage house Cantor Fitzgerald and it dragged on – sapping senior management time and attention – for almost five years. In the end it was another unsuccessful attempt to get one over the competition – Telerate and Bloomberg.

Cantor Fitzgerald provided Telerate with what Reuters saw as the Holy Grail – a feed of what were widely regarded as the best inside market prices of US Treasury securities. Reuters had chased round for years trying to get an equivalent feed. One marketing manager, Ivan Mulcahy, had even persuaded senior management to invest in a reporting unit that would attempt – by phoning around brokers and dealers – to create a 'live' alternative to Telerate's feed. But in practise this never worked because there is no such thing as a 'live' quote unless a trader can deal on it.

Drayson, who had been previously president of the broker-age house MKI Securities, thought he could go one better. He accompanied Ure to a meeting with Cantor Fitzgerald's CEO Howard Lutnick, who had a reputation for being able to cut through stone with his eyes. Lutnick had initiated the meeting but insisted on seeing an executive director – hence Ure's involvement. Their discussions led to the proposition that if Cantor Fitzgerald could not give Reuters US government bonds, perhaps it could provide an alternative and equally important feed of Japanese and other non-US government bonds? They struck a deal, and negotiated and signed a contract. Then, quite quickly, things began to unravel.

The ten-year deal was arranged through Market Data Corporation (MDC), which did all the data vending for Cantor Fitzgerald. A former Reuters manager, Scott Rumbold, who had been an early pioneer of Reuters business in Latin America but had jumped ship to Telerate, was hired by MDC as executive vice-president to manage the partnership.

The feed went live in late November 1993 and within a few months Reuters was arguing that it was not getting what it had contracted to pay millions of dollars for. Lutnick disagreed and claimed he was fulfilling the contract. People familiar with the Cantor Fitzgerald side say that, from their viewpoint, it came down to Reuters exaggerated expectations.

"Reuters expected an all singing and dancing feed the next day and Cantor thought they could produce it pretty fast."

"It had taken Cantor Fitzgerald ten years to get a really full feed of US Govs up and running for Telerate – the break only came when Merrill Lynch agreed to put up their prices. Five years was probably a more realistic time-frame to develop a full feed of Internationals and Japanese for Reuters," one source close to the deal said. "It started as a trickle but apparently Reuters was expecting, or banking on, a stream. In the end the time frame envisaged by both sides was too optimistic. Reuters expected an all singing and dancing feed the next day and Cantor thought they could produce it pretty fast."

Reuters challenged Cantor Fitzgerald. An arbitration clause in the agreement was invoked and Reuters was set for another US legal roller-coaster that lasted nearly five years and involved hundreds of senior management hours. It became virtually a full-time job at Reuters for Drayson, who had been hired not to file law suits but to find new markets. Thereafter he never had a good word to say for Lutnick – neither did anyone else at Reuters.

Watching from the sidelines, another former Reuters manager, John Jessop, could only smile. Jessop had joined Reuters as an office boy in 1959 and, after leaving as a successful sales manager, had risen to become chief operating officer of Telerate. Jessop knew Lutnick well.

"It was an awful contract. The lambs of Reuters were sent to the wolves of Cantor Fitzgerald."

"It was an awful contract," he said. "The lambs of Reuters were sent to the wolves of Cantor Fitzgerald. The contract never spelled out what Reuters was going to get. They had only themselves to blame and I am surprised that Ure survived."

Drayson disagrees and says Reuters knew precisely what

they should have been getting. "The fact is," he says, "we negotiated one hell of a deal and I can't think of any other company
that beat Lutnick over fifteen rounds."

Glocer was by then Reuters in-house lawyer in New York
and played a big part in bringing the arbitration to settlement,
particularly towards the tough endgame. Some $200m was at
stake. Cantor Fitzgerald sources say the settlement was "very
much in Reuters favour", but Reuters still paid a high price in
having to go all fifteen rounds.

**"It distracted senior management for several years . . . It was
immensely disruptive and a concentrated loss of professional
time."**

"It distracted senior management for several years and was
eventually settled on very satisfactory terms to Reuters," one
Reuters insider says. "But there were many depositions. It was
immensely disruptive and a concentrated loss of professional
time."

Ure was observed by one colleague sweating over legal
depositions in his office on Boxing Day. "It effectively took his
brain out of circulation for twelve months," the colleague says.

Ure even today recalls his experiences of the US legal system with something approaching anguish. "They were as
unpleasant as it is possible to imagine," he says.

The Cantor Fitzgerald and Levkoff cases exposed a fundamental weakness of Reuters position in North America. It had
been operating as a business in the US since the 1970s but,
compared with its American competitors, still only had a tiny
share of the huge domestic market.

Starting on the back foot, Reuters was therefore always seeking to buy its way into market share and, as it was learning to its cost, what you see in the US is not always what you get.

VAUGHAN'S VISION

Brian Vaughan, a British accountant who had cut his teeth with Reuters in Latin America in the 1970s, was one of Reuters first managers in the US to appreciate the importance of growth in the domestic market. By the time he took over as president it had some 2,000 employees in the Americas.

Reuters was also beginning to see off Telerate – then its biggest rival in both the US and the rest of the world. Telerate had thrived for years on its Cantor Fitzgerald feed but had not renewed its technology and could never match Reuters in foreign exchange, dealing or news. Telerate relied on Dow Jones for news and it was this relationship that would ultimately kill it. Dow Jones acquired full control of Telerate in 1990 and quickly discovered that it would need to spend up to $600m to put the company back onto a war footing with Reuters.

"There was mutual incomprehension from the outset . . . It was the worst marriage imaginable."

"There was mutual incomprehension from the outset," says Jessop. "Telerate was a lively, entrepreneurial organization while Dow Jones was a very conservative, august, editorial-driven company. Dow Jones simply did not understand online business and dealing rooms. It was the worst marriage imaginable."

Dow Jones initially bit the bullet and announced a major

investment programme to rejuvenate Telerate, 'Rolling Thunder', which old-time Teleraters nicknamed 'Strolling Blunder'. But the new mother company lost its nerve and CEO Ken Burenga lost his job. Telerate withered. Jessop thinks this was bad for Reuters.

"Reuters just slipped into arrogant complacency."

"As soon as Telerate had gone," he says, "Reuters just slipped into arrogant complacency."

Vaughan did two big things. He bought the failed equities vendor Quotron from Citicorp, which overnight gave Reuters a large domestic client base. He also had a Vision, which was his undoing.

Many of Vaughan's supporters still argue that his Vision was the right way to go – a programme to get all staff in RAM (as Reuters Americas was known) to buy into a sense of common business purpose. Reuters globally was now generating huge profits, and revenues were at last growing in North America. Vaughan matched this by rolling out new offices in the Midwest, West Coast, Texas and Florida and strove to give RAM an American identity.

All 2,000 staff were sent on three-day 'awareness-building' meetings at locations such as Palm Springs or Amelia Island. Technicians, secretaries, journalists and managers mingled, wrestling with mission statements and, by many accounts, each other. But perhaps the most controversial element was a new appraisal system which involved managers being evaluated by their own staff, something Head Office in London found distinctly uncomfortable.

"We talk about it as a change process," Vaughan told an interviewer at the time. "The Vision is a very strong catalyst for change in our organization. There is a tendency for people to think we should be going around having experiences around Vision. But the idea is to open up the organization."

The opening up part involved the controversial 360-degree appraisals. Marty Wolk, who spent a decade at Reuters as a correspondent in New York and Seattle, recalls the 1990s as a time when crafting vision statements was all the rage in corporate America.

"RAM went full bore into this corporate charlatanism."

"RAM went full bore into this corporate charlatanism," says Wolk. "The culmination came in 1993 when every single RAM employee was invited to a 'Vision conference'. This included secretaries who probably never even filed an expense report for a taxi ride in their life. They broke us up into four groups. At least two of the conferences were held at The Registry, a super-posh resort in Naples, Florida, with golf courses, tennis courts and alligators in the lagoon. One afternoon we had time off and the company paid for our choice of a massage, herbal body wrap or facial. Later we went skinny-dipping in the Gulf of Mexico, and there were reports of a drunken midnight brawl on the golf course. And who knows who ended up in which room at night?"

"I don't think the movement ever really caught on in London."

"We were forced to work in intolerable hotel ballrooms till

past midnight, arguing over Vision words in small groups with sales execs and software developers and, at the end, the consultants came up with a convoluted Vision statement for RAM that was embossed onto little cards we were supposed to carry in our wallet. I don't think the movement ever really caught on in London."

That is an understatement. The Vision undermined Vaughan's credibility and he was first shunted out to San Francisco to run the West Coast and Latin America then, soon afterwards, was sacked altogether. He was replaced by the head of Instinet, Mike Sanderson, an ex-Merrill Lynch trader, son of a Luftwaffe bomber pilot, who had been brought up in the trouble spots of the world by a stepfather who was a US secret service agent.

CONFIDENCE CRISIS

Mike Reilly believes legal challenges in the US in the 1990s seriously undermined Reuters confidence, helping bring about a growing aversion to risk that was in marked contrast to its bullish expansionism under Renfrew.

"Particularly at board level, there was just shock and amazement that such a thing could happen."

"The shareholder law suits filed in 1992 – so-called strike suits or class actions – had a dramatic impact," says Reilly. "Particularly at board level, there was just shock and amazement that such a thing could happen, that the suits could be filed. In

English law you don't see that sort of thing, but over here – ten a day."

There were originally two suits against Reuters combined into one, brought by 'strike lawyers' who make a living filing suits against corporations. They monitor trading in stocks and, if a share moves more than 10%, they look for evidence that something out of the ordinary and, in the litigious culture of the US, potentially actionable might have caused the move.

"They have been known to file suits actually before they have done their homework, and then go and look and see if they could find something, and make allegations that the company did wrong," Reilly says. "Over 80 or 90% of the time they settle out of court, which is their aim to begin with."

"They settled for a little over $6m, but the actual costs had to be at least twice that."

"These suits were over Dealing, allegations that the company misled people about the prospects for the Dealing 2000-2 matching service. Ultimately it was settled out of court. There was no finding of any sort. The company did exactly what the lawyers were expecting. They settled for a little over $6m, but the actual costs had to be at least twice that."

"We had teams of people coming into the offices of our developers, engineers, sales people, anyone connected with Dealing, in this country, England, Japan. Teams of lawyers would come in and you were required by law to hand over your files, which included examinations of hard disks, and transcriptions of every paper you had. Plus lawyers' fees while they were doing it, then depositions, getting on a plane to come over here, for five or six years."

"When that first set of law suits was filed, there was such a tremendous feeling of shock and anger that we could be accused of acting that way. Sir Christopher Hogg's name was on that first law suit and I think that caused an amazing shock wave. The lawyers said: 'Now say almost nothing about your prospects or any product prospects while you are going through this process, dealing with this action', so they pulled back in their public statements. But I think it also meant and felt like a pull back in the entire strategic activity. To me that was really the essential point when the company seems to really change. It lost its nerve, it lost its energy for innovation."

Reuters legal troubles in the 1990s never seemed to go away. The company was also dragged into a major tussle with the Australian Tax Office over a £25m claim and even the roll-out of a new editing system for the company's journalists sparked a law suit.

If all that wasn't enough, Reuters suffered one further embarrassment in the US at the end of the 1990s. A senior British finance executive met an untimely end in a New York hotel room. He was wearing women's underwear and had ingested large amounts of cocaine and alcohol. He had also been in the company of two prostitutes, one a transvestite, who had reported his demise. His portable computer contained confidential financial information from Reuters, as well as the addresses of S&M parlours around the world, and there were thousands of dollars in cash in his briefcase.

Reuters went to great lengths to hush up the scandal and

protect his identity. One senior American executive involved says the incident neatly highlighted the cultural chasm between Reuters British and American managers: the British were shocked by the drugs and the Americans by the cross-dressing.

4

Shooting for the Moon

I can tell you in one word what went wrong with Reuters," says an analyst who has tracked the company for more than a decade: "Armstrong."

Project Armstrong was born out of the failure of Decision 2000 and exceeded in complexity and ambition anything Reuters had ever done. It was technically the most challenging undertaking in Reuters history. The objective was to create a third pillar to the business, to add databases to the existing real-time feeds of prices and news and create a brand new platform on which to provide financial services that integrated all three. Reuters was going to reach out to the future and build an entirely new generation of services and products. This was to be Job's defining legacy and Ure's crowning technical triumph. Armstrong would not merely kill Bloomberg but, this time, totally bury it.

"I can tell you in one word what went wrong with Reuters: Armstrong."

By 1993, Bloomberg had become something of an obsession in Reuters, although at this stage it was still dismissed by many in top management as old technology serving just a small market niche. "He was regarded as an interesting phenomenon at that time, but not one that was going to eat our lunch," a senior marketing manager recalls.

Bloomberg's feed of real-time money rates was limited and its news service, although winning plaudits, was not as comprehensive, fast or reliable as Reuters. Moreover his platform was closed in an environment that was going increasingly open. But this did not stop traders from liking, even loving, their Bloombergs, which provided them with tips on buying shirts and wine and, in an age before e-mail had become standard, enabled them to communicate via its messaging facility. Bloomberg had created a community, and, above all, it was easy and instinctive to use – a feature that was now being acknowledged in the most surprising places.

"It was so easy to operate," says a former Reuters marketing manager. "I remember sitting at a dinner across from André Villeneuve, and he had had an hour on a Bloomberg terminal that day and was staggered by the ease with which he could find his way around the Bloomberg product."

Reuters answer would be Armstrong. Ure oversaw the project and one of Job's favoured inner-circle from Asia, Jeremy Penn, was handpicked to lead it. Penn read English at Oxford and had joined Reuters in 1981 as a graduate marketing trainee. He worked in business and marketing roles in Southern and North Africa before heading East to join Job's thriving Asian empire, where he rose effortlessly and, by all accounts, on merit, to become head of equities marketing. Now in his early thirties, he was seen as a good 'bulldog' manager who would get the job done, and he was already talked of a possible successor to Job. But his judgement on technical issues was not considered flawless and his detractors were quick to recall his support for the ESL graphics solution. Penn had a fair degree of technical appreciation but no specific technical qualifications. He was about to lead a major project that was 90% technical engineering.

Armstrong began in 1993, like many initiatives emanating from Ure with a big budget and in the utmost secrecy. The name was chosen at an inaugural meeting of a team of developers and marketers at a London hotel. An American at the meeting recalls how his British counterparts had drawn parallels with Neil Armstrong's 1969 moonwalk.

"The moon programme was held in high regard by our British colleagues. The idea that President Kennedy set a target – we're going there in a decade – and then, with all the amazing teamwork and resources, actually did it. With our British colleagues it resonated."

One of the early decisions of the group was to outlaw the word project. Armstrong was officially to be known as a programme. It was too big to be a mere project, although over time its more humble sobriquet survived.

Databases have high value in the fixed-income and equity markets. They enable financial professionals to perform vital fundamental analyses such as valuing securities, making investment decisions and managing their portfolios. But building databases was a major challenge to a company that had hitherto mostly thrown away its data. Reuters had until now thrived on 'real time' – the latest prices in the money and equities markets, and the latest news. Little of this information, until relatively recently, had been saved and neither Reuters programmers nor its technical centres were equipped to handle or store what was seen as essentially dead data. Reuters had acquired and not made much use of one major database, IP Sharp in Toronto, and was in the middle of a muddle over acquiring or replicating another – Levkoff's CMD in Stamford. Its primary textual database, Textline, contributed to the project with background data on equities.

Creating databases called for an entirely new culture. Databases involve storing and being able to interrogate thousands of millions of prices and permutations; it is a huge job to build and maintain them. Bloomberg had constructed his business around the database he had already created. He then added on real-time news and prices. Reuters was now trying to do precisely the reverse – to build and add on a database to its real time feeds. This was a technically far more challenging proposition, especially as Reuters had little knowledge or experience of the engineering characteristics of relational database systems, nor how traders actually used such data.

Between June and October Penn organized a series of off-site meetings at which great lists were drawn up – the design and development of big databases, a new network that would eventually replace IDN and a new suite of applications. The products were divided into two – equities and fixed income.

By October 1993 the specifications had been boiled down to

more than 2,000 pages of complex technical text. Later on, the project plan was drawn up and a paper copy covering some 30 square feet was pinned up outside Penn's office on the fourth floor of 85 Fleet Street – the old Editorial headquarters. The display was widely viewed as incomprehensible. In 1996, it eventually collapsed onto the floor under its own weight and was left there and trampled under foot until somebody binned it.

The plan was to build the equities part of the new system from scratch while fixed income would come from Levkoff's former company in Stamford, now owned by Reuters and renamed Reuters Analytics. Hubert Holmes, who had borne the brunt of the fallout with Levkoff, was put in charge of fixed income, and Penn took charge of the equities side.

Crucially at this early stage neither data content nor its use by financial market users was discussed in any depth. Penn had hired Unique Consultants to do some primary market research of the buy and sell side, and to analyse the strengths and weaknesses of Bloomberg. Much of this work drove the initial specifications.

Nor was there any specification for delivery of the product by datafeed, which was an increasingly important part of Reuters business. The product drove the project from the very outset and, like an uncontrollable leviathan, in the end the product took control. There were tensions throughout between members of the Armstrong team, who saw technology merely as a means of delivering content, and the self-styled 'trekkies', who believed Reuters future lay in technology products such as Triarch. In the end bodged technology prevailed and nowhere did Reuters more tellingly prove to be product driven, rather than customer driven.

FLYING CIRCUS

But it would not just be a simple leviathan; it was to be multi-headed. Armstrong began life with two main geographical bases – London and Stamford – and with several outposts – Colchester, Toronto, Tiverton and later Prague – and with two separate bosses, Penn and Holmes. Both reported to Ure.

"It was never really clear who was in charge."

"It was never really clear who was in charge," says one former Armstrong executive. "Jeremy and Hubert divided up the job for producing these things politically. The whole thing was driven by politics."

"The fudged reporting under Ure, of Penn and Holmes, cannot be underestimated in its effect," says a senior technical manager. "No one was in charge of the programme. In addition no one was in charge of the overall technical architecture, as there had been with IDN, other than Penn who was not technically qualified to do the job."

The user interface, which would be the most visible thing about the product – the touchy-feely bit that people got to see and use – was divided into two pieces and carved up between Stamford and Colchester, where Reuters had a development subsidiary, Equisoft.

"You could not imagine a more complicated arrangement."

"In the end neither had the lead. You could not imagine a more complicated arrangement," the former executive said. "Stamford wanted to do fixed income all alone. There were huge tensions. In the end the project took twice as long to complete and cost four times as much as budgeted."

"It was a flying development circus."

He calculated that in one year alone there must have been more than 1,000 return business class flights across the Atlantic. "That's £2m squandered on travel and on exhausting staff. Every two weeks a team of fifteen software developers whose job was to programme the pages that sat on top of the Equisoft core would fly from Colchester and Stamford. They ended up exhausted and with no productivity. It was a flying development circus."

This was well into the project in 1995, when the Stamford and Equisoft staff rebelled and refused to work with each other. In response, a SWAT team was set up with developers from both centres. They were all given bomber jackets with SWAT on their backs.

"At one stage we tried to co-locate. But Ure bluntly refused saying: 'You've got the phone, you've got e-mail'." Nearly ten years on, he still defends the decision, saying: "I would be amazed if that had any negative impact".

The flying circus did not just involve Stamford, London and Colchester. Developers also shuttled back and forth to San Diego to work with NCR on the Teradata machine, the engine room of the database. And later, there were flights to and from

Prague. British Airways and Marriott hotels did well out of Armstrong.

Dean Ratcliffe, an economics graduate from Manchester University with a background in working with and building financial databases, was recruited in 1994 specifically to work on Armstrong. He recalls a meeting in Stamford in which he realized that everyone present had flown there from London.

A northern England grammar school boy from Wigan with spiky hair, Ratcliffe was a different cut from the normal 'suit'. Most of the London-based Armstrong marketing team were in typical English style, like the Civil Service, intelligent generalists. Several were Oxbridge, including an Eton scholar. Two had a background in oil and energy and another had worked in M&A for Reuters. None was really an equities specialist and they were altogether completely different in style from their more down-to-earth North American counterparts in Stamford.

Most of the developers had a background in real-time rather than databases. Ratcliffe had started out as an auditor at Price Waterhouse where he quickly developed an aptitude for building systems and working with databases – skills that took him to CountyNatwest, Paribas in Paris and Boston, and then to Reuters.

"As an end-user I absolutely hated Reuters and I had heard so many bad things about the company, but I went along to a breakfast with Jeremy Penn. I had all the database skills they desperately needed and in the end I got on quite well with Penn and agreed to work for him."

Ratcliffe was in for a shock on his first day in the early summer of 1994. Penn had disappeared for a week, and Ratcliffe found himself working alongside a 22-year-old graduate trainee who had been given the task of helping coordinate the data functional specification of the database. The trainee reported to someone whose background was in real-time data.

"It was a right balls-up from the very beginning."

"He told me they were aiming for a test version by August – this was in May and they hadn't yet completed the data functional spec. There was a Visual Basic prototype but no data. There was no way that the data and product could have gone into test phase and gone live by the year-end. In truth, these people hadn't got a clue. It was a right balls-up from the very beginning."

It was not long before Ratcliffe had to come to grips with one of the fatal flaws in Armstrong – NCR's Teradata 3600. In technical terms this was a huge data warehousing machine that was massively parallel, massively relational and massively scaleable. It had been bought from NCR 'almost over a weekend' after models proposed by DEC and other vendors had been found wanting.

The Teradata machine was then being used by a major US store chain, WalMart, and provided an impressive array of information about stock levels, orders and sales. But nobody involved with the decision at Reuters seemed to question whether this would be an appropriate system for real-time, second-by-second interrogation by busy traders across the globe.

"It was the wrong tool for the task."

"Teradata was hopeless for two reasons," says Ratcliffe.

"Firstly when you interrogated it you never knew how long it would take to come back with the answer, and secondly, it could not do joins, so none of the relational properties ever functioned. It was the wrong tool for the task. Teradata is fine for a data warehouse, but totally unsuitable for a production system with lots of updates."

Apart from major problems with the so-called SQL join, it was quickly found that in order to get performance, a lot of the processing capacity of the machine had to be spent on 'denormalizing' the files. The entire database had to be recalculated every night as the developers were under so much pressure that it was quicker for them to do this than make everything event-driven. Because of the timescales it was decided to leave the databases on their original sources or homes, and copy the data to the Teradata machine. This meant that loading new information or, for example, adding a new field to the database, such as cash flow data, involved not just one but several distinct operations. Anything changed on the Teradata database also required a change in the original source and the feeds between them.

To save time and costs, part of one of the equity databases was transferred from Logica in Brussels to Logica Prague, but the move ended up costing more money and adding to the confusion. Reuters English-speaking project managers had problems communicating with the Czech programmers, and they in turn had a steep learning curve catching up to the point where the Brussels Logica programmers had handed over.

Each Teradata box cost $15m and the Armstrong team ordered three to allow for incremental use as new products took off. This was in accordance with the company's technical policy, TP102, which states that there must be enough capacity to handle all potential users plus spare capacity. The figures used to justify the purchase were based on forecast sales rather than usage, and because eventual usage of the database was so low – less than 10% of subscribers – the extra two Teradata boxes were never used to their full capacity. Long before that was evident and in a dreadful augury for the future, the first one blew up when it was installed at Reuters gleaming technical centre in London's Docklands. Fire sprinklers doused its fan, which was overheating, and it was out of action for months.

There are many accounts of how Reuters came to rely on a database machine best suited for a supermarket. The most consistent version is that it came down to a decision by Buford Smith – one of the rare occasions when his daring approach to new technology seems to have failed the company.

"This was right at the leading edge and it was always going to be a tough battle to get the beast to function," a senior technical manager involved in the decision recalls. "It was a leap of faith that Teradata would do the job. We were striving to build a perfect database. The clinching argument for Buford was that it was based on standard PC technology. The argument was superficially a sound one, that leveraging the cost reductions in PC technology would benefit long term. The home-brewed nature of the manufacture negated this."

The problem in the end was not so much Teradata itself, but the use to which it was put. Some of those involved on the technical side still argue that the Armstrong design was at fault in not taking into account the basic architecture and therefore the limitations of the machine. Teradata was originally bought to be used as a data warehouse and would probably have been useful in that role. This would have let Reuters move data from the IBM mainframes in Toronto and close Toronto down – as had been planned for years.

If there were problems in Armstrong's engine room, things were not much better at the user end.

"Teradata was a bad flaw."

"Teradata was a bad flaw," says one of the senior Americans working on the project. "But the giant flaw was not using industry standard IP technologies and browsers – Internet technology basically. But at the time Internet technology was in its infancy as far as commercial use, and you were unsure of security and unsure of delivery guarantees, unsure of performance guarantees. That mattered a lot."

After careful evaluation comparing industry-standard Excel and Equation, a software produced by Colchester-based Equisoft, Equation was selected – by a narrow margin. This turned out to be another unfortunate decision. The main problem with Equation was that it was a real-time calculator that was good for calculating options in real time, but was not really suited to front-end a database. It wouldn't run over a network and was slow to load, and because of the language that it used – Equiscript – it was hard to find anybody who could programme it.

"It was an awful piece of code, and ran like a dog."

"Equation from Equisoft was all wrong," says one of the

core team members. "It was an awful piece of code, and ran like a dog." He is similarly dismissive of the graphics system used. "The charts were from ESL, whose code was by then in care and maintenance. They looked horrible."

The actual user interface was little better. It was designed by Human Factors International from Iowa and they came up with a solution for viewing quotes and news which they called the 'Tablet'. Everyone agreed that it was not very pretty.

Then came the knockout blow. In August 1994 it was decided – with Ure's approval – that the Tablet would only be used for viewing historical reference data and analysis. The existing Reuters Terminal would be retained for the display of quotes and news. This meant there would be two applications running on the same screen which both took several minutes to load, and which only talked to each other through 'a clunky and inelegant' Reuters-designed protocol called RACE. This was a far cry from the original objective for Reuters to deliver its new state-of-the art products on one single viewer, which was what Bloomberg had always achieved. There were protests that this would confuse the user, make it hard to find data and seriously slow down the user's PC.

"Armstrong and Reuters never fully recovered."

"The RT decision was a defining moment in the project," according to one key insider. "The goal of an end-user experience to rival the Bloomberg was sacrificed on the altar of technical expediency. Armstrong and Reuters never fully recovered."

Development continued with more and more impossible

targets and, as specifications chopped and changed, Armstrong started to give birth to new clones – an open desk-top version, Moonraker, which Penn subsequently renamed Discovery, and a client site database system called Viking, which Penn barred from accessing Reuters new database on the grounds that it might cannibalize terminal sales.

As concern mounted about the depth and breadth of the new databases – they were thought by market experts on the team to be too thin and superficial – a crash programme of 'waves' was instigated promising a series of new releases every hundred days. Staff in Stamford and at Equisoft in Colchester, meanwhile, all but stopped working together because Stamford developers complained they did not want to work with Equisoft's Equation. Stamford people were database developers with skills in Visual Basic and C and they considered learning Equiscript a waste of time.

A key milestone was a planned demonstration of the product to senior management in May 1995. It took three months of critical development time to set up but, in the event, it was a partly canned demo because there was not sufficient data on the Reuters database at that stage and developers had to create a data set to feed the demonstration. As the development stage neared completion it was discovered that some of the analytics had been produced three times – in London, Stamford and Colchester – and that all three were different and wrong.

Version 1.0 of the first product – spawning Securities 3000, Treasury 3000 and Money 3000 – limped out of the door in late 1996. The culmination of three years development effort by 500 people, it had cost at least £150m, but it was slow and complicated and did not do much. Reuters' big business centres threw huge parties to celebrate the launch, but the response on the ground was one of crushing disappointment.

"The sales force was bitterly disappointed. And they now faced the challenge of selling and getting installed a product that most clients did not want."

"The sales force was bitterly disappointed," says a business manager. "And they now faced the challenge of selling and getting installed a product that most clients did not want."

Securities 3000 soon ran into a wall of indifference, particularly with third-party trading room vendors, because there was no integrated real-time data in the user interface, and there were no options. But at least the product was fed by the new Reuters database. Treasury 3000 relied on the old Stamford database and on its own front end. Money 3000, on the other hand, did not make use of any databases and was, in effect, solely a real-time product. It was a technical and product mess on an unimaginable scale, and resulted in users needing three separate products to cover the markets. Sometimes it would take a minute to fire up one of the applications just to get a price or quote. Nothing could have been further from the original concept of an all-in-one, easy-to-use, single screen solution – which was exactly what Bloomberg offered.

Moreover, the product was expensive both to install and to maintain. Each client needed a server, which then cost around £10,000, and two data lines. Most customers ignored the database side and just continued using it like an old RT. There was hardly any activity on the database – client retrieval statistics were embarrassingly low.

But most damaging of all Reuters had saddled itself with a big beast for its flagship products which required intensive technical support and distanced the end-users – the traders – yet further from the company. A new version, Reuters 3000Xtra, gradually emerged from the wreckage with integrated applications that actually talked to each other – thanks to the use of software from Paris-based Effix and its Kobra workstation.

But what the company called this 'Premium desktop' was in effect the 'mother of all workstations' requiring extensive installation time and a lot of field technical support, and sapping huge capacity from the end-user's terminal. As a result, Reuters relationship with its customers became increasingly one of IT-based solutions rather than the provider of what the end-user actually wanted to see.

"There was a lot of sealing wax and string behind it all – and they are still trying to unpick it all."

A senior technical manager who saw the product through to launch was similarly scathing. "Armstrong carried a lot of risks, as the company was buying an off-the-shelf database, and also an off-the-shelf IP communications solution. It took a long time to build and did not work as well as hoped. The front end desktop was clumsy, with two applications which did not talk to each other. A lot of knitting together took place at the desktop – there was a lot of sealing wax and string behind it all – and they are still trying to unpick it all. There was an 80/20 thing going on with the end product – most users only used 20% of the product's capability."

In fact the majority of clients were not using any of the new pieces. It was more like a 100/0. A senior American executive says the contrast with Bloomberg, which was instinctive and easy to use, could not have been greater.

"You could see that it had been stitched together whereas what appears on a Bloomberg screen is married to the end-user's expectations."

"The biggest flaw was that two applications had to work together," he says. "You could see that it had been stitched together whereas what appears on a Bloomberg screen is married to the end-user's expectations."

Peter Sharrock, who took on a new role as international director of customer focus at about the same time as the launch of the 3000 range, was shocked by initial customer feedback.

"The first report I came out with was a bombshell. It went right through the company, and it had major customers saying 'This product is crap' within months of the launch."

"The 3000 product was one of the first things I did customer interviews on," Sharrock recalls. "The first report I came out with was a bombshell. It went right through the company, and it had major customers saying 'This product is crap' within months of the launch."

David Gandy, a senior business manager on the sales front line for many years, says Armstrong was released far too early.

"It was never complete. It was a product designed by Reuters, not by clients."

Senior management panicked and the product was shovelled out to achieve targets that Job had set. Several country managers cut corners by counting the installation of a server as an installed unit – even though no one was using it. Sales had to cut prices and carry the costs of installation and the technical upgrades – anything to force customers to take it. Estimates of how much net new revenue Armstrong earned the company were a mere fraction of the £150–250m it spent on the programme.

The initial disappointment was perhaps not surprising. Most first versions of complex financial service products start their lives as less than perfect and then are progressively enhanced and improved. But with the hope and expectation of building on it, disaster struck. There was total management change and the Armstrong team was effectively disbanded. Penn was sent to run Asia, a move widely seen as a reward for getting a product out at all, and John Parcell took over responsibility for the programme.

Close colleagues say Penn in retrospect sees his move to Asia as a mistake. He left the project when it was still in its cot, where he believes Parcell effectively finished it off. The colleagues say Penn is otherwise unrepentant and feels 'very strongly' that as a development programme it was 'very successful'. They say he got the product to phase one, to base camp.

Penn does, however, concede to colleagues that using Teradata was misguided, "the source of most of our difficulties". But he maintains that this was a technical decision largely out of his control. He also acknowledges that Equisoft was the wrong choice.

"The company did not spend enough. In the end we took three years and delivered crap."

"What should have happened is that we were given three years and told to go away and do it properly," says one of the Armstrong team members. "Building databases is an expensive business, like building a news service. You are talking about investing huge sums, billions, over many years. This was a totally different sort of cost structure and the company shied away from completing the job. There is a high fixed cost, and a high entry cost. The company did not spend enough. In the end we took three years and delivered crap."

Another team member says the project was an ill-conceived attempt to catch up with a competitor and there was too much pressure on Penn to deliver something – anything, in the end – quickly.

"The real problem with Armstrong was that the whole thing was done under time pressure. Instead of a new group going away and building from scratch it had to build using a lot of legacy systems – and with Reuters expecting to release a product within twelve months," this member says. "Bloomberg took years to build his product and it was designed by somebody who was from the market, building for the market. Previous to Armstrong other Reuters ventures such as Monitor, Dealing and IDN had been innovative, whereas Armstrong was a poor copy of an existing system."

PASS THE PARCELL

John Parcell was first of a breed – a Reuters journalist who had excelled as a correspondent and then risen high in management. Previous journalists-turned-mangers, notably Job and Ure, had not shone as journalists. Parcell was a cut above. He had reported the downfall of Phnom Penh and Pol Pot's takeover of Cambodia with distinction, although perhaps in later life regretting that he had not made more in his reporting of the brutality of the incoming regime. After further foreign assignments, including Mexico, Parcell joined management, with a marketing role in the successful launch of IDN. He could never claim the technical accolades for the project, but he had put down his marker. In October 1990 Parcell was named manager of the UK and Ireland.

He inherited an administrative mess and bequeathed one of the best-run business operations in the company. This was his passport to a seat on the board. Reuters had grown at a phenomenal pace in the 1980s, with many countries adopting their own management and accounting information systems. The culture was 'sell, sell, sell', and very often sales staff did not even have to do that. Orders just came in over the telephone. There was very little client and business management and the result was chaos.

Parcell was brought in to sort out the mess in Reuters home market, which he did by effectively building the business again from scratch and dividing it into four highly efficient divisions. He ordered sales staff to resell every service to their clients and created a customer-orientated business. He also developed and launched a successful UK equities product, Reuters Equity Focus. In 1996, he was rewarded with responsibility for information products – which accounted for 60% of the company's revenue including all the products emanating from Armstrong – and with a seat on the board.

Penn's view, largely corroborated by those who worked with Parcell, is that he took over Armstrong and did nothing with the project for two years. Parcell's former colleagues say this was because he realized he had inherited a product that was going nowhere. Penn's men say it was because he wanted to turn in good figures and so refused to spend any more on development.

"He basically canned all existing projects, all existing plans, produced nothing for two years and then generated the Kobra-based 3000Xtra, which was a project that was already well under way under us," says one of Penn's team. "We had started that project as part one of the alternatives to Equation. But I don't think Parcell even got his head around the existence of that project for 18 months."

Parcell in effect slowly let Armstrong version 1.0 wash away with the tide to return as the more successful Reuters 3000Xtra, but the drive to build databases, the strategic rationale for developing Armstrong in the first place, just stopped.

Why was Parcell so concerned with his figures? The answer lay in Geneva, and across the boardroom table. Jean-Claude Marchand, an engaging former salesman for Bernie Cornfeld's Investors Overseas Services, had worked his way up through Reuters to head continental Europe, headquartered in Geneva, with a seat on the board. Marchand, a Swiss, ran what was regarded as the slickest and by far the most profitable territorial operation in Reuters. The technology he backed usually paid dividends and, although he was by no means an intellectual, his easy-going style combined with his ability to turn in good results year after year made him – at least in his own eyes – a serious contender for the top job.

Job was by then obsessed by his succession and, in his anxiety to ensure that the right man succeeded him, set up Parcell and Marchand to fight it out for his job. They seem to have despised each other and the feud between them, far from resolving the succession issue, created a fissure deep inside the company.

"Geneva hated Parcell with a passion. This really tore the company apart."

"Geneva hated Parcell with a passion," says David Gandy. "This really tore the company apart. The feuding between (Parcell's) Reuters Information and (Marchand's) Global Sales was a disaster. Parcell and Marchand did not talk to each other. They could not stand each other and literally at times refused to be in the same room."

"They were like two dogs fighting over a bone," says Hans Ouwerkerk, who spent much of his career working closely with Marchand. "In the end, a third one came along and pinched it."

A former senior manager who reported to both men at different times concedes that there were problems – Parcell, for example, refused to attend Marchand's Infoworld biennial exhibitions of Reuters products in Geneva, which drew clients from all over Europe. But in public, he says, their mutual antipathy rarely revealed itself. "After all, it would be a disqualification from consideration for the job of CEO to be seen bickering with your chief rival."

But, he concedes, "day-to-day relations between the two

management camps were not easy. There were no serious attempts to obstruct one another but, equally, there was little sense of working towards a common goal."

He dismisses suggestions that Parcell washed his hands of Armstrong, saying he put serious effort into developing what would become 3000Xtra. "Parcell invested heavily in additional development staff and in data analysts," he says. "He was ambitious for the top job. It is inconceivable that he would have deliberately scuppered his own new flagship product."

Short termism became not just the order of the day, but an obsession. As part of his campaign to persuade the board that he was their man, Parcell set out to deliver better figures than Marchand. He drew up a five-year plan for information products, canning as much investment as possible. Penn's supporters believe he thereby sacrificed Armstrong.

"Armstrong was abandoned under Parcell," concedes a former close colleague. "Parcell at that point was basically concerned only, as were all the board, with the succession. The normal thing with a big product programme, for example when Bloomberg came out with his initial product and subsequent variants, almost always the first pass was very weak. That is normal. You get something to first base and it is a model which you then develop and go on improving."

FEDERAL FIASCO

By the beginning of 1998, project Armstrong had been quietly pushed aside and development of its legacy product, 3000Xtra, was under way. Peter Job, as he surveyed the company from the seventh floor of the newly refurbished head office, could look back on the previous year with satisfaction. Reuters would be posting pre-tax profits for 1997 of £626m and giving £1.5bn of its cash pile back to shareholders, and was planning to build a new headquarters for its American operations in New York's Times Square. Then in January some stunning news broke: the FBI was investigating Reuters.

The investigation centred on Reuters offices in Stamford, Connecticut where Hubert Holmes was now president of Reuters Analytics, the company he had helped forge out of the failed partnership with Levkoff. In an undercover probe that had begun almost twelve months before, the FBI was investigating allegations that Reuters may have been stealing data or source code from Bloomberg.

The news sent shockwaves through Reuters and spawned gruesome newspaper headlines around the world. The share price crashed as analysts tried to quantify the threat to Reuters reputation and business; the launch of a US version of Securities 3000 was imminent and might have to be put on hold. The enormity of the situation sank home fast and Job realized the company's very future could be at stake. Reuters hard-earned reputation for integrity and trust was under question.

The FBI had begun its investigation early in 1997 after being alerted to unusually high downloads to a Bloomberg terminal at the offices of Cyberspace Research Associates, a consultancy in New York run by a former Bloomberg employee, David Schwartz. An FBI special agent investigating computer crime, Dave Marziliano, was assigned to the case and before long a trail had led him from Schwartz's office to Reuters at

Stamford. The big downloads of Bloomberg pages were being printed out and couriered up in boxes to a marketing or data department there. The FBI planted an agent at Stamford, bugged the Reuters offices and began to assemble evidence for what looked set to turn into a major case of international industrial espionage.

Mary Jo White, who had just taken over from Mayor Rudolf Guiliani as Attorney for the New York Southern District, decided she had a potential case under the US Economic Espionage Act of 1996. This had stemmed from the trade secrets case pursued by General Motors when one of its vice-presidents, Jose Ignacio Lopez de Arriortua, left to join Volkswagen, taking with him a bundle of confidential documents. VW eventually paid General Motors $100m in cash and agreed to buy $1bn in parts from GM over seven years to settle the matter. Congress subsequently passed the Economic Espionage Act which made stealing trade secrets a federal criminal offence. The Reuters Analytics case looked a potentially serious case of computer espionage, and sources close to White's office said the authorities were initially talking in terms of arresting Job or Ure if they set foot in the US.

Reuters clammed up, except for one interview in February in which Job told the *Wall Street Journal* it was 'possible' one of his staff might have done something wrong in trying to compete with Bloomberg. Job stopped short of accusing anyone of wrongdoing but, asked whether employees might have committed crimes in trying to catch up to Bloomberg, said: "Anything is possible."

"If, in the course of doing comparative analyses, and trying to improve our products and services, we have improperly used certain Bloomberg proprietary information, then we, as an ethical company, will take appropriate steps to fix the problem."

Job issued a statement clarifying what he had told the *Journal*. "We, like our competitors, try to compare the performance of our products and services to those of our competition. We have not viewed these kinds of assessments to be illegal or improper. Indeed, we believe they are essential to promoting competition and serving the needs of our customers. If, in the course of doing comparative analyses, and trying to improve our products and services, we have improperly used certain Bloomberg proprietary information, then we, as an ethical company, will take appropriate steps to fix the problem."

Reuters sent Holmes, Jeff Walker, the head of fixed income marketing, and one of Walker's staff, James Feingold, home on paid leave, and Job dispatched one of his old Asian lieutenants, Geoff Weetman, across the Atlantic to take command at Stamford. This was not the first time Holmes had been involved in a potential law suit. It was Holmes who had sparred with Levkoff in 1993 for control of CMD, which was then folded into Reuters Analytics. Not surprisingly, Levkoff was keen to talk to the FBI and says he gave them an 'uncompromising view' of what he thought had happened.

A Federal Grand Jury was appointed and the affair dragged on for eighteen months with Reuters future on a knife-edge as the jurors heard and deliberated over evidence from dozens of witnesses to determine whether or not there was a case. Everyone involved at Reuters – more than thirty people – hired lawyers, all paid for by the company. More than a dozen law firms were involved and the legal expenses alone ran into millions. At least one senior executive even hired his own detective.

One Stamford insider dismisses the affair as "the biggest misunderstanding of all time. Much like Ford looks at Chevrolet, this is part of what good marketing and research are all about."

"Jeff Walker's team was studying the competition in multiple ways and they got this consultant David Schwartz to look at it. He had a Bloomberg. He was hired to study Bloomberg, basically. Really at a high level, features, benefits. It was the most harmless of things."

He insists any suggestions that Reuters Analytics was trying to use Bloomberg data or copy or obtain or reverse engineer its source codes or algorithms were totally unfounded, and says top people at Bloomberg also concurred that this had nothing to do with the code or algorithms.

"I think that they would compare Bloomberg data with our data and if they did not match they would do some research to find out why. They certainly would not have just put Bloomberg data in, because it wasn't deemed to be particularly correct or accurate itself."

"So Bloomberg went out and saw some consultant that had some connection with Reuters. We were not hiding anything – just standard competitive research. And he said: 'Holy shit! They are stealing my data! They are stealing my stuff!' And so I think he called the FBI. Their computer crime division got involved and they thought that conceivably we were doing something. They thought it was a British company that was stealing the industrial secrets of a US company and that kicked in the Industrial Espionage Act, which is a very serious thing."

"It escalated beyond comprehension."

"It escalated beyond comprehension. So everybody got lawyers. The upshot was that we showed definitively that the actual code and the algorithms we did not want, and did not use. We were doing our own development and we showed that. We also showed that, by definition, all these algorithms were in the public domain. Everything in the Bloomberg is public stuff, and the deals with the public securities markets. The analytics and all that stuff was just a *non sequitur*."

"On the data side it was also wrong. The data wasn't going into the [Reuters] database. I don't know what was being done, but I am sure it was just this comparison thing. And then, of course, Bloomberg is openly available in many public places."

"At one stage a low-level Reuters guy was asked by a prosecutor in front of the Grand Jury if he thought Reuters use of Bloomberg was wrong, and he explained that, since you could access Bloomberg in all these public places such as airports and libraries, he felt fine about his marketing work. Then an individual Grand Juror said: 'Hang on, do you mean to say that all these supposed secrets we have been told about by the government are freely available in public?' The whole thing just started to unravel. The US Government did not understand the securities business or the financial data business – they made a big mistake."

In July 1999 it was announced that the case would not be pursued.

"I think it changed the way people study their competitors. It was quite an experience."

"I think it changed the way people study their competitors," says the Stamford insider, who has since moved on from Reuters. "It was quite an experience."

The experience left Reuters deeply shocked and raised internal questions about management control. Had Stamford, with a staff of over 300, been adequately supervised? Mike Sanderson, still president of Reuters North America, complained that he did not know what was going on at Stamford, just forty minutes from his downtown New York office, because the operation reported to London.

A close associate of Holmes says he strongly refutes any suggestion Stamford was not properly managed. It was part of international marketing and Holmes had a clear reporting line to Ure and, as head of capital markets marketing for Reuters America, another direct to Sanderson. He was in regular contact with both men and others in top management.

"It is simply not true to say that Hubert and Jeff were not supervised," the associate says.

Reuters responded to the news that federal prosecutors had decided against filing charges with 'gratification'. Its conduct throughout the investigation had been meek. There seems to have been no attempt to advance the 'publicly available' defence before it came out in front of the Grand Jury.

Bloomberg's retaliated with an uncharacteristically hostile statement, saying: "The fact that the prosecutors and the FBI took over two and a half years to evaluate whether the evidence would satisfy the very high burden on the government of proving beyond a reasonable doubt that Reuters committed a crime is a powerful indication of how serious the allegations were. Based on information available to us we believe that Reuters, in an effort to design a competing product, obtained improper access to the Bloomberg System and to Bloomberg's proprietary information."

Bloomberg also said that the decision by the US Attorney's office to close the investigation "should not be viewed as an endorsement of that behavior".

Bloomberg for a while contemplated a civil suit but this threat receded and so – at least in public statements – did Reuters ambitions to go head-to-head with or 'kill' Bloomberg. Compliance lawyers meanwhile took an ever-closer grip on the business and Reuters became even more risk averse.

5

The Jewel in the Crown

News is Reuters lifeblood. The company's reputation for accuracy, reliability, independence and trustworthiness is built upon it. News has been at the heart of Reuters almost since its inception and is still what most people associate Reuters with; it is Reuters calling card.

And yet Reuters had never made much money out of news and for many decades the news services scarcely generated sufficient income to guarantee their future, surviving more or less from hand-to-mouth, and with the occasional soft government subsidy. It was the imperative to preserve the independence of news that led Reuters to seek alternative income sources to, in effect, subsidize news and guarantee its continuity and freedom.

Gerald Long used to enjoy telling the heads of state-backed news agencies, such as France's Agence France Presse, Italy's ANSA and even East European Communist agencies such as PAP of Poland that, whereas they could rely on government funding, Reuters had to find alternative business streams to fund itself and maintain its independence. This was a key factor in the decision to launch services like Stockmaster and Monitor.

The unexpected runaway success of Monitor and subsequent services such as Dealing transformed Reuters into a global multimedia player and enabled the news services to flourish. In the space of twenty years, Reuters launched more than twenty foreign language news services, and pushed aggressively into television, radio, photos, graphics and news on the Web.

But ironically, the runaway success of financial services and the drive into technology eclipsed the news services in the eyes of many senior executives. News began to account for less and less of the company's overall revenue – less than 10% in the published accounts, which reflected only revenue from media clients since financial news services, with the exception of regional and local language services, were not billed separately.

On this basis, and compared with the rest of the business, news looked high cost and low margin and its direct contribution to profits was almost zero. But internal Reuters estimates of revenue attributable to editorial in the 1990s ranged between £340 and £430m, with about two-thirds of this down to financial news services. With editorial costs running at a little over £200m it looks in reality like a comfortably profitable operation, so why downplay it?

This was the paradox on which news operated in the modern Reuters, and which led to editor-in-chief Mark Wood leaving the board in 1996. He was replaced by Parcell and Marchand, who would both claim they were bringing in the revenue and the profits. The inside news story of the last three decades was that of searching – almost entirely in vain – for a pot of gold and for big profits from news services. Only with the Internet and the spread of Reuters news across the Web did that Holy Grail ever come into view.

Editorial methods changed rapidly as the computer technology that was transforming the business also revolutionized newsgathering and dissemination. At the beginning of the 1970s incoming news stories in the London newsroom were distributed to newsdesks in trays fired along ceiling rails by catapult. Copy was 'pencil-subbed' or rewritten on ancient typewriters and finished copy went from editors to the teleprinter operators along slow-moving belts, in slots graded according to urgency. "Snap in the belt," a desk editor would call as a major newsbreak trundled slowly down the conveyor. Journalists in the field would punch their stories onto tape and transmit them on slow-speed wires. But by the end of the 1970s every newsroom and most bureaux were equipped with computerized video-editing terminals and a newsflash would go from an editor's screen to clients' printers or Monitor terminals in seconds.

By the 1980s, AP and Dow Jones were providing news for Reuters biggest competitor in the financial markets, Telerate, and competition between the rival news services was intense. Breaking news such as a major economic indicator, interest rate change or political development could move markets dramatically in an instant, and even a 'beat' of just a few seconds over the competition was regarded as a coup.

Prior to the advent of Monitor, Reuters financial journalists were very much the poor relations of their colleagues on the general news desks, regarded by some of the older World Desk hands as little more than glorified clerks. They were a proud lot, the general news men, and, indeed, had every right to be so. They were responsible for the world's most respected news service, and from their ranks had sprung writers such as Edgar Wallace, Ian Fleming and Frederick Forsyth as well as generations of top newspaper and broadcast correspondents and editors. Even today Reuters continues to breed international best sellers such as Britain's Tim Sebastian and Iain Pears and prize-winning French author Éric Faye.

The gulf between the two sides of editorial was enormous. True, there were financial journalists in major bureaux around the world, but the bureau chief jobs always went to General News men. As a result, many financial journalists left for greener pastures with better long-term career prospects. Reading the bylines in the *Financial Times* was like looking through a Reuters old boys directory.

When Michael Reupke became editor-in-chief in 1978 he determined to break down what he saw as an unnecessary and damaging division. Reupke was also keen to decentralize editorial and to foster more closely targeted regional news services, both for media and Monitor clients.

In 1983 a new desk was set up in Bahrain, to coordinate coverage of the Middle East and edit both general and financial news services for the region – the first 'bisexual' desk in Reuters modern history. Although the regional editor was from a general news background, the desk was headed by a financial journalist, an appointment viewed with suspicion by some senior World Desk men.

It worked well, financial reporters and sub-editors from

both sides of editorial switching effortlessly from financial and oil market stories to the Iran–Iraq war, aircraft hijacks and Middle East politics. Reupke's successor Mark Wood, who took over in 1989, continued the policy and, within years, correspondents around the globe, with the exception of a few specialists, were expected to be able to report with equal facility for both media and financial services.

Under Wood, more and more local language services were set up to provide domestic financial news to screen clients alongside the international markets news. This helped consolidate the financial information screen services and created a significant degree of subscriber loyalty. The breadth and scope of Reuters financial and domestic news was a key selling point and also, increasingly, helped ward off the threat from the upstart Bloomberg News.

But Wood never succeeded in getting the company accounts presented in such a way that the revenue from these financial services was separately listed. That meant the only easily identifiable news revenue was from so-called traditional media – primarily photos, television and general and sports textual news.

MILKING THE MEDIA

Peter Job had always been proud of his editorial background, but enjoyed a paradoxical relationship with editorial, mistrustful of journalists, regarding them as anti-management, even disloyal, and rarely mixing with them. But he had taken deep offence when a venerable former correspondent-turned-manager, Vergil Berger, remarked once after a drink or two: "Peter, I will never be as good a manager as you are, but I was a bloody sight better journalist!"

In Asia, Job had pressed his managers to extract more revenue from media clients and when he took over in London, he determined to make this a global policy. He tasked a succession of senior managers – Enrique Jara, Hans Ouwerkerk, Geoff Weetman, Phil Melchior, Rob Rowley and Jeremy Penn – with delivering the results.

Newspapers were the principal market but had no growth prospects. Newspaper circulations were declining and many newspapers were becoming more parochial and less interested in foreign news.

The British press continued to pay only nominal rates for the news service, a hangover from the days when they had owned Reuters. Titles like *The Times*, *Daily Telegraph* and *Guardian*, making extensive use of the service for their foreign coverage, were paying just a few hundred pounds a month. The national papers together were barely paying enough to cover the cost of one foreign correspondent – often £100,000 a year or more including salaries, housing, overseas allowances and office and other expenses – while having access to the output of the hundreds of correspondents Reuters was maintaining around the globe.

A new pricing structure was drawn up, based on detailed analysis of the papers' use of the service and their circulations, with a premium rate for the qualities per thousand circulation and correspondingly lower rates for the mid-market and tabloid titles. At the lower end of the market the increases were minimal, but the qualities faced massive price rises from absurdly low historical rates. Most, after a few weeks of resistance, grudgingly accepted that the increases were justified and signed up to the new contracts.

Only the *Daily Telegraph* held out. Reuters refused to back down for fear of undermining a now generally accepted pricing policy, and so too did the *Telegraph*, opting to replace the Reuters service with that of Agence France Presse. It sent shockwaves throughout Reuters, but also the *Telegraph*'s own staff. Alec Russell, then a correspondent, now the Foreign Editor, says he and other correspondents were dismayed that they would no longer have access to the Reuter file. Job and UKI managing director John Parcell stuck to their guns, however, continuing to maintain that the policy was right and that the *Telegraph* would eventually return to the fold as, indeed, it did a couple of years later – although at a far lower subscription.

Another battle erupted with the Press Association, Reuters former owner. For years the PA had paid Reuters substantially more for the right to use its foreign news in the PA service for regional papers than Reuters paid to use PA's domestic coverage its overseas services. In 1991, with the contract due for renewal, the PA argued that the two services should simply be exchanged.

But the PA was facing mounting discontent from clients dissatisfied with its service. Reuters saw the opportunity to launch a rival domestic service and approached the dissidents. Parcell was initially sceptical but, when the regionals reacted positively, threw his weight behind the project, bringing the executive committee with him into what promised to shape up as a major conflict between the agencies – with considerable political overtones given the PA's importance as a conduit to the media for politicians of all shades.

Reuters drew up detailed plans to launch a competitor service, putting together a comprehensive package which included domestic coverage, local sports results, horse racing, TV listings and a plethora of other information it had never covered before, much of it to be preformatted for page-ready delivery in individual newspapers' house styles. At the last minute Thomson Regional Newspapers, the key player among the PA dissidents, backed away. The PA survived and Reuters plan folded. There were other tussles with European news and photo agencies but none quite as acrimonious as this, and the smell of cordite hung over the joint offices of Reuters and the PA at 85 Fleet Street for many months. It was about this time that Reuters decided to buy the PA out of the building and refurbish it.

For Reuters it was a lost opportunity that could have considerably broadened its range of media services. For the PA, it was a both a dramatic reprieve and a wake-up call. Chief executive Robert Simpson rapidly transformed the PA to meet its clients' needs more closely and diversify into new areas, embracing new technologies. "It made a better company of PA," Simpson says.

Reuters fared better in its battle with another news agency across the pond – United Press International (UPI). By the 1980s this once great American wire service was in its death throes. UPI had a broad US client base but no financial news arm to help defray the costs of global reporting, and Reuters virtually finished it off by knocking it out of many of its domestic

US subscribers, including the *New York Times*, and then by buying up its photo service. Reuters bought its non-US pictures business in 1985 and launched its own news pictures service, its first serious venture into photojournalism and a valuable complement to the textual news services.

But this was no pot of gold. Reuters had bought an old crock, and the entire photo service required a massive injection of funding to provide new cameras, dark rooms and transmitters. The service chalked up a loss of £6m one year against revenues of only £4m, and Wood had to fight hard to keep it running. Reuters was discovering that a good picture may be worth a thousand words, but does not come cheap. Editorial had traditionally avoided big spending but suddenly it was hiring helicopters to get photographers to disasters. The photo service required another major upgrade a few years later as the technology switched to digital. It has attracted top news photographers and won many plaudits, but never made enough money to excite Reuters bean-counters.

Reuters also spent a considerable amount in the late 1980s developing a news pictures terminal, to store a limited number of pictures digitally with basic editing features. Although only capable of handling black-and-white pictures, it was better than anything else then available. But it, too, turned out to be a bad investment. It was rapidly superseded by Adobe's Photoshop software, launched in 1990, which quickly became the standard in the Apple Mac-dominated newsrooms of the world.

In another attempt to strike profitable media revenue streams, Reuters plunged into historical news databases. The company had a numeric database, IP Sharp, in Toronto and in

1986 bought a UK-based company, Finsbury Data, whose Textline database provided clients with subject-coded abstracts and full versions of newspaper and specialist magazine articles over a cumbersome dialup interface. Textline eventually evolved into an easy to use Windows-based product, Reuters Business Briefing, and armies of coders were deployed first in London, then in Tiverton in southwest England and other parts of the world such as Barcelona as more publications and non-English language sources were added to the database.

Reuters had to pay royalties to the thousands of publications included in the database and, while use of the service grew steadily, there appeared to be no economies of scale – every time revenue went up, so did the sales costs.

Reuters database was also relatively weak on US news sources. Its long-term rival Dow Jones had a similar system, strong on US content but weaker on non-US news. In 1999 the two got together and merged their databases into a Web-based service under the name of Factiva. The 50–50 joint venture significantly enhanced both the range of available news sources – 8,000 publications worldwide and a similar number of business websites – as well as broadening the client base, which reached 1.5m by the end of the millennium. This was a mass audience compared with Reuters traditional wholesale client base and was part of a long-held ambition to reach out for a larger so-called lower-tier market. After a £4m loss in 1999, Factiva was contributing £5m to Reuters bottom line by 2002. But it was still small fry – a huge effort for a tiny profit – and nowhere near the scale originally dreamed of.

TACKLING TV

Reuters attempts to make money out of television were not much more successful. In 1992 Reuters took full control of Visnews, the international television news agency based at Park Royal in the northwest suburbs of London, previously jointly owned with the BBC and NBC of the US. Reuters had originally acquired a small stake in Visnews as far back as 1960, trebling it to 33% in 1968 and upping it again to 55% in 1985. Nelson's view, he recalls, was that Reuters "should either get out of it or take it over, because I thought that any self-respecting news-gathering organization that was not in television was missing out on the future."

"Any self-respecting news-gathering organization that was not in television was missing out on the future."

Even after Reuters acquired the majority, Visnews remained to all intents and purposes a separate entity. Many in Reuters were unaware of its existence and, even in overseas bureaux, contact or cooperation between Reuters correspondents and Visnews crews was limited.

When it took full control, Reuters seemed to have little idea of what it wanted to do with Visnews, which was renamed Reuters Television (RTV) the following year. Its managing director Julian Kerr was quietly shipped off to Australia to be replaced by Enrique Jara. But, while he was a former journalist and long-serving Reuters manager, Jara had no experience in television and the rationale for his appointment, or so it seemed to many in the upper echelons of Visnews, was his long-standing friendship with Job, dating from the latter's early career in South America.

Visnews' flagships were its international satellite feeds of news footage, which offered separate services for different continents and regions. These were provided in 'natural sound', with no commentary or on-camera correspondent, but with accompanying scripts to enable television clients to dub their own voice-over in whatever language they chose, or to edit the footage in with their own or material from other sources.

The Visnews library was another major asset, a vast archive of more than 25,000 hours of footage dating back to the earliest days of moving pictures – grainy old black-and-white pictures of Queen Victoria and Kaiser Wilhelm picnicking together, dramatic footage of wars, famines, disasters and great events – an invaluable pictorial record of the late nineteenth and twentieth centuries. Its problem was that it was held on every film and video format known to man in a labyrinthine warehouse at Park Royal, with only a card index catalogue.

Opportunities for development were plentiful. Newly developed digital TV technology was becoming a commercial reality, offering huge cost savings in satellite distribution and the ability to distribute video in real time over terrestrial networks.

In principle it was simple. A single frame of analogue video converted to a digital image represented more than one megabyte of data – about the size of a floppy disk – so, at 25 frames per second, this was 25 MB or more of data per second — an impractical amount. Digital compression software, however, was able to analyse the differences between one frame and the next and transmit only the changes. This dramatically reduced the amount of data that needed to be transmitted, error-checking every few frames to make sure it was getting it right. By the early 1990s that 25 MB datastream could be compressed down to 3 MB with substantial further improvements in prospect.

For the RTV news service, this technology presented the opportunity to slash delivery costs by switching from expensive analogue satellite channels, to far cheaper digital satellite segments occupying much less bandwidth.

It also offered the possibility of upgrading services to parts of the world poorly served by satellite delivery. In the Middle East and Africa, for example, RTV clients had only a few feeds of video daily via an analogue satellite which required a huge tracking dish to receive the signal. This meant they were reliant on local PTTs to receive the feed – invariably an expensive option. Digital offered Reuters the chance to provide a 24-hour, broadcast-quality service direct to small dishes at the clients' premises and, in many cases, save them money. The first digital service was launched for the Middle East and Africa in 1995, significantly boosting client numbers and revenue as well as the quality of service, and other areas were quick to follow.

Not all opportunities presented by digital were seized, however. One was digitization of the RTV library. Researchers seeking footage for documentaries or other programming would have to travel to Park Royal to view potential material, wait for a tape or take the footage on trust. But digitization could enable them to search through a vast digital catalogue, view the material for suitability in low resolution from anywhere in the world and, if it matched their needs, confirm and pay for the order and receive the broadcast-quality material either on-line, or by digital satellite or on tape.

It was an ambitious and costly idea – well over £10m, but hardly earth-shaking for a company of Reuters size. Potential revenues were hard to assess, but certainly such a system would have opened up a vast new market, making the RTV library without question one of the most important in the world, easily accessible to a far wider potential client base. Instead, Reuters rejected the plan on cost grounds, dithered for a couple of years over what to do with the library, then handed it over to ITN, in which Reuters had a minority shareholding, to manage for them.

The big challenge was a 24-hour global news channel. As early as 1992 a proposal was drawn up for a financial TV news service, replicating in digital video what Reuters had for so long done so successfully with textual news. As with the traditional news services, the plan was for editorial control and content to pass from region to region, Tokyo to London to New York in a 24-hour cycle, a mix of financial news bulletins, breaking news, market updates, announcements of key economic indicators, interviews and analysis as well as general news and sport.

The primary market would be the hundreds of thousands of dealers in the world's financial markets sitting with Reuters terminals on their desks, who would now also get digitized video through a TV window on their screens. Not, of course, that they would have watched it round the clock. But, as Reuters did with news flashes on major stories, dealers could be alerted to upcoming video potentially of interest to them through textual alerts, in time to open the video window and watch it live.

Other possible sources of revenue would be distribution via the growing global network of satellite and cable channels and 'stripping rights' sold to other broadcasters, allowing them to use the RTV material in their own programming.

Ted Turner "used to lie awake at night worrying about whether Reuters would launch a news channel".

Wood also considered a CNN-type news channel, or a mixture of general and financial news. Buoyed by its success in covering the first Gulf War, CNN International had become highly profitable, and one top CNN executive told Wood that he and the channel's founder Ted Turner "used to lie awake at night worrying about whether Reuters would launch a news channel".

Wood, though, found little enthusiasm for the idea of a news channel among his colleagues on the executive committee and board. Job's view was that Reuters should not start competing with its customers. It was, after all, making lots of money providing TV news footage to the 24-hour news services like CNN and Sky, as well as hundreds of other TV newsrooms around the world.

There was also a brief flirtation with news programming by regional managers – financial news programmes in the newly liberalized eastern European countries and elsewhere, a weekly news magazine in Africa – but most quickly foundered on lack of central management support.

A financial news channel was another matter and very much Reuters legitimate domain. CNBC was the only serious financial channel, though very American-oriented. Supported by

Carlton Television's Michael Green, then a non-executive director of Reuters, Wood continued to press for the launch of Reuters own financial channel. Here was an opportunity to propel Reuters into a new media age with a service that exploited all the company's traditional strengths – the technological power and resources to deliver the financial market expertise of 180 news bureaux around the world to a global television audience that was keener than ever before on investment and markets news.

The rest of the board and executive committee continued to prevaricate and in 1994 a half-baked compromise, Reuters Financial Television, was launched. Rather than a continuous service, it provided regular morning and evening briefings and the occasional injection of press conferences, interviews or other financial news direct to the TV window on the RT. Reuters put a marketing spin on the service. This was not the wallpaper television that flickered away in the background in every dealing room but was not really watched. This was finely targeted and timely broadcast of stuff dealers would want to drop everything to watch.

Big bonuses were in play to ensure the service was rolled out to clients and initially it was sold separately. But in some cases the charges came nowhere near even matching the expense of installation – a separate satellite dish and cabling – let alone the costs of production, and eventually, as fewer and fewer clients watched the service, it was dropped altogether. Reuters Financial Television became the most expensive and perhaps least watched television in history.

Bloomberg Television became the ultimate triumph in Bloom-

berg branding, and everywhere Reuters' subscribers, staff
and executives went they saw it.

And who should pop up with a 24-hour service, just two
years after Reuters had first looked at and then rejected the idea,
but that man Bloomberg again? At first, Bloomberg Information
Television really did look like wallpaper and had few regular
viewers, but little by little, wallpaper caught on and it was
pushed out into trading rooms, banks, offices, reception areas,
airports, stations and over satellite and cable to homes and
hotels. Whether or not it made money did not matter.
Bloomberg Television became the ultimate triumph in Bloomberg branding, and everywhere Reuters subscribers, staff and
executives went they saw it.

For Reuters it was a big miss – in branding, if not in
bottom-line business. Failure to grasp the nettle with a 24-hour
financial news channel was a bad mistake, symptomatic of the
risk-aversion and lack of entrepreneurial drive that had set in by
the mid-1990s when the drivers were now altogether more to
do with shareholder value. Although Job had previously been a
strong proponent of media and editorial, he seemed to lose
interest while other board and executive committee members
had long been at best ambivalent, and in some cases antipathetic
towards media. FX fixation was at play again. Media projects,
with a longer investment payback than for financial market
products, simply did not offer high enough returns to excite the
board and senior management.

Another factor was an ill-fated venture into radio. Twice in
the early 1990s Reuters had bid for new radio licences to launch
a news channel but lost out to other bidders. In 1994 it bought

London News Radio with its two LBC frequencies. Parcell was the prime mover behind the acquisition. LBC had had a turbulent past, and the acquisition was initially viewed as something of a bargain. One of the two frequencies was a talk radio station, which Reuters left pretty much alone, focusing instead on its main 97.3 FM service and pouring money in to develop it as a news channel.

Reuters had no experience and no real understanding of radio, and failed to listen to those who did.

Finance director Rob Rowley had set demanding targets for the venture, and it rapidly became clear these were unlikely to be met. According to one senior editor involved, Reuters had no experience and no real understanding of radio, and failed to listen to those who did. It threw too much money at the project, building up staffing to absurd levels, but spending a pittance on advertising and promoting the channel.

Job was not amused and, just a year after the station's relaunch, rumours were circulating that Reuters wanted out. Harrods' owner Mohamed al-Fayed expressed interest, but John Major's Conservative government quietly let it be known to Reuters that a sale to the controversial Egyptian would not be viewed favourably.

One of the country's biggest radio operators, GWR, was brought in to help revamp the station and in 1996 Reuters sold most of its stake to GWR, ITN and The Daily Mail & General Trust. Reuters finally managed to sever all links with LBC only in late 2002, when it sold its remaining 20% to Chrysalis Radio, which also bought out the other partners – only after a takeover offer from Bloomberg Radio was rejected.

Senior executives involved in the venture say it soured relations between Job and Parcell and prejudiced Job against further efforts to expand Reuters media interests, undermining Wood's efforts to build a coherent media strategy. In 1990 he had become the first Reuters editor to sit on the board, but in 1996 he departed in a boardroom reshuffle to make way for Parcell and Marchand.

Officially it was said the Trustees had become concerned that Wood's involvement in discussions of Reuters wider commercial interests might jeopardize editorial independence. But in truth, there was little point in him being there since, by this stage, the board rarely discussed media issues. In the summer of 2002, Wood left Reuters to become executive chairman of ITN.

Even though he ultimately failed to build a viable media business strategy, Wood had consistently and successfully defended editorial budgets and, as a result, the quality and strength of the news services remained unaffected by the crisis in the rest of the company. In fact, the more its fortunes on the business front declined, the more Reuters sought to emphasize its leading international role in news and the lasting qualities of its newsfile and the values underpinning it.

Reuters multimedia coverage of the 2003 war in Iraq which, like conflicts in every corner of the globe down the decades added to the toll of Reuters cameramen and journalists killed in action, was universally praised. Bloomberg, by contrast, came under fire in the press for using a Baghdad dateline when it had no staff there. Reuters had eighteen staffers in the Iraqi capital and another thirty-three 'embedded' with the invasion forces.

The company has drastically slashed staff levels in response to the sharp downturn in its fortunes in the past couple of years, but editorial has not yet been hit hard. The number of journalists has held at around 2,000 while total staff was being cut from over 19,000 at the end of 2001 to a target of 13,000 by 2005.

Daily Telegraph foreign editor Alec Russell says Reuters "remains the first agency that we consult" with no sign that it is slower or less reliable than in the past. Comparing it with the competition, Russell says Reuters still exercises "better judgement in what is a news story and what isn't".

His opposite number at the *Guardian*, Ed Pilkington, agrees that there has been no sign of the service's quality suffering, though he adds that the file is 'not great' out of the US. That, though, has long been a problem given the strength of the AP file on its own turf and the breadth and depth of its domestic coverage.

In financial news Reuters also remains dominant – although only just. Bloomberg's news service is snapping at its heels and now employs almost as many news staff as Reuters – 1,500 journalists and editors worldwide. Bloomberg's news is widely regarded as 'less stodgy' than Reuters, although Reuters has come a long way in encouraging its journalists to report in a lively manner, provide more analysis and write in the everyday language clients can relate to. Every major customer survey of the past ten years shows customers citing news as the most valued part of Reuters product offering, and loyal clients say it has undoubtedly help stem the tide of cancellations.

118

"When the last Reuters screen is switched off – if that ever happens, there will still be a Reuters news service out there."

Few doubt that whatever happens to Reuters core financial business the news services will survive. "When the last Reuters screen is switched off – if that ever happens," one analyst commented, "there will still be a Reuters news service out there."

One area where Reuters news business really took off under Wood was on the Web – but this was thanks to an initiative that sprang entirely from one or two individuals in the US.

6

Dotcoming

More than anyone else, it was a college drop-out and former UPI journalist who led Reuters into the Internet Age. The push came in the US, but surprisingly, it came from a sector of Reuters where senior management had long ago concluded there would be no more growth and certainly no innovation – from media. Andy Nibley showed them they were wrong.

After quitting college, where he was studying English and philosophy, Nibley started out in Washington with UPI and moved to Reuters as treasury correspondent in 1980. He progressed swiftly to become a senior editor, in both London and New York, before moving into a more business-focused role when, on 1 January 1994, he teamed up with Buford Smith to co-found Reuters NewMedia. Smith was president and Nibley executive vice-president, and it developed into an inspired partnership. Nibley believed passionately in marketing while Smith was equally hooked on new technology.

"Long after American civilization is over," says Nibley, "long after they have forgotten about getting to the moon, air travel, cars, whatever, America will be remembered for one thing – marketing."

Nibley had early on in his career at Reuters understood the power of branding. He had helped kill off his old wire service, UPI, by getting Reuters news into 200 newspapers across the US. In one early instance, he defied senior managers by doing a deal with Ted Turner in which he dropped the price for the Reuters television service in exchange for a Reuters credit every time CNN International broadcast an RTV news clip.

"At the time I was derided for giving away stuff that cameramen had risked their lives for, but over time they saw that this was the right way to go. Branding is everything. We started to win new business from people who didn't even know we were in the television business."

Smith was a technology pioneer whom Ure describes as 'Reuters great guide to the Internet' and 'a remarkable man'. Apart from inadvertently lumbering Armstrong with a database more suitable for a supermarket, he seems to have had an almost infallible instinct for frontier technology, particularly at the client end. He had risen to become head of global technology under Renfrew and was largely responsible for moving Reuters to PCs and satellite delivery of services. His relationships with Intel and Microsoft were critical. He saw the potential of the WinTel powerhouse before most Americans, let alone the rest of the world. He was also instrumental in the purchase of Teknekron, from which Reuters made a lot of money, and under his leadership at NewMedia, Reuters made investments in

Yahoo!, Infoseek, Digimarc, Sportsline and other similar companies. He was fired in 1996 after telling the executive committee that they would not recognize a telex machine if it came at them.

"Buford was frustrated at their fear of technology," says Isaac Piha, the top finance vice-president at NewMedia. "He felt that if they had been running the company when telex, or even the automobile, was invented, they would have run the other way."

Nibley's genius was to see an opening for selling Reuters news on the new websites that were now sprouting. Reuters pushed its news onto hundreds of portals throughout the 1990s, totally eclipsing its rivals and converting Reuters into a household name for millions. In 2000, at the height of the dotcom boom, the company estimated its content was seen by 73 million users a month on 1,400 different websites.

Revenues from new media quickly surpassed traditional media in both the US and UK and new media ventures took off in dozens of countries around the world. The boom was short-lived, though. The dotcom bubble burst and the bulk of the revenue quickly evaporated as expiring client contracts were not renewed.

Nibley, though, had shown Reuters the way to a mass consumer market but Job, now mid-way through his ten-year term, and the company generally seemingly did not want to know. In the mid-1990s Reuters had a chance to reinvent itself as an Internet company. But this did not happen. Nibley recalls London's frequent scepticism.

"The message from Head Office in London for years was:

'Don't mention the I-word in public. We don't care about consumers. We are for business professionals.' We were trying to put Reuters on the map in America and it was discouraged all the way. We were seen as American marketing cowboys, fast-talking American bullshit.

"Meanwhile, the biggest marketing, fastest-talking cowboy of them all, Michael Bloomberg, was branding away, buying radio and television stations, putting up billboards all over New York, buying the right to put his name on the outside of the blue rain bags that covered the home-delivered *New York Times*, basically kicking our ass.

"NewMedia was seen by a lot of people as this funny ship of fools. All the people who were loud and obnoxious and said the company needed to move faster, they put us all in one boat and pushed us off from shore. We were as surprised as they were when we came back with gold, silks, spices, nuts.

"Then one day they shut NewMedia down. There was a story in the papers, saying the new media unit was closed. This was in 1996 when the Internet was just taking off. I told my people this had to do with getting rid of Smith. They were going to melt us back into the core business.

"I told my people: 'This is a big multinational corporation. They don't even know what building we are in, much less what floor we are on. They will never find us and will keep paying us. Just keep on doing what you are doing and if our strategy is right, we'll look good in the end.'

"Two years later I am on the analysts' tour with senior management explaining what a great Internet strategy we had."

Ure insists that Reuters was quick to see the possibilities of

the Internet and equally quick to exploit them. But not everyone agrees, and they point to major missed opportunities.
Under Smith and Nibley, Reuters had picked up a stake in
Yahoo! for virtually nothing, then sold over half the holding for
a very low price.

Then along came an incredible deal in which Steve Case,
founder of AOL, offered to take a loss-making personal finance
Web-based service, Reality, off Reuters in a win–win deal.
Reuters would pay him $10m (just $2m more than Reality was
losing each year) and in exchange would receive a 10% stake in
AOL, which at one point was worth almost $16bn. Reuters
executives who worked on the deal recall Job saying he thought
on-line was an American fad and that in any case he did not like
the name AOL.

He was equally dismissive of a business plan to launch
Reuters main financial services onto the Internet, saying
Reuters was not a telecoms company; and as late as 1995 he said
Internet was just for geeks.

The Yahoo! investment was half-hearted. Reuters made
Yahoo! by giving them quotes, news and TIBCO in exchange
for advertising revenue – but commercially the company only
put a toe in the water.

"Job was fixated on Reuters being a B2B business," says
one American manager. Job's indifference to or ambivalence
towards the Internet was not an isolated case. The entire executive board seems to have shared his views, at least early on.
Smith and Nibley organized a dinner for the board at New
York's Museum of Radio and Broadcast soon after NewMedia's
foundation. The guest list read like the 'Who's Who' of the new

economy – AOL's Steve Case, Jim Clark of Netscape, Jerry Yang of Yahoo! and Nicholas Negroponte of MIT's Media Lab.

"Buford pulled together all these people," Nibley recalls. "But the board was not impressed. 'Who are these people?' they were asking. We were very much discouraged."

"Reuters had the foresight to form one of the first Internet companies and one of the first profitable ones at that. But the company never really knew what it had created, and senior management spent a lot of time deriding and criticizing their own child."

"It was a shame in many ways. Reuters had the foresight to form one of the first Internet companies and one of the first profitable ones at that. But the company never really knew what it had created, and senior management spent a lot of time deriding and criticizing their own child."

Like many of his contemporaries Nibley, who later achieved success in both the music and advertising industries, looks back at his time with Reuters with mixed feelings. "I loved working at Reuters. It was an amazing company of very bright people. But once it got to be immensely successful in the financial services business, it seemed to lose that entrepreneurial spirit and drive that had made it great in the first place."

Mike Reilly, in charge of investor relations in the US, recalls a similar collective put down over the Internet and also believes this was consistent with the fact that the entrepreneurial spark and pioneering spirit left Reuters early on in Job's time as CEO.

"I remember talking to a couple of board members about this issue of going to the Internet," says Reilly. "I was knocked down very hard indeed, and one executive director said perhaps there was some opportunity in the corporate communications field but we would never find an opportunity for our business services. There was no brooking any discussion whatsoever."

MIXED METAPHORS

For most of his time as CEO Job did not have a strategy – or at least he did not feel the need to articulate one. Indeed, he seems to have taken pride in having no strategy. He made a number of public speeches early on in which he proudly proclaimed that his strategy was not to have a strategy. Reuters was operating in such a fast-moving and turbulent world that any strategy you could devise would become outdated anyway, and that it was preferably to be have a more flexible approach.

He explained his reasoning in an interview in 1994 with Walter Wriston, the former chief of Citicorp, and one of the first non-executive directors brought into Reuters from the business and banking world.

"I believe in analysing skills, but not in sweeping strategies or vision statements," Job told Wriston in an interview for the US publication *Chief Executive*. "The problem is that if you formulate a vision, conditions change, and your statement becomes outdated. That confuses everybody. You shouldn't have a strategy unless you're not going to change it for ten or twelve years. That's how long it will take to realize it.

"Our strategy today is what we think today, and tomorrow it will be what we think tomorrow. We change our minds. We change direction. We're flexible. That's the key."

So, just like his speeches, which he often changed at the last minute, Job would make it up as he went. "Let a thousand flowers bloom," he once said.

On another occasion, he told senior managers that Reuters was like an echidna. He was fond of intellectual conceits and, as he had intended, the managers went scurrying for the dictionary, where they may not have found much enlightenment. The *Concise Oxford Dictionary* defines echidna as an "Australian toothless burrowing egg-laying animal like hedgehog, spiny anteater".

"I think what he meant was that we were supposed to be a small nimble animal darting about opportunistically," a senior marketing executive says.

The result was that for almost all the Job years, the focus in Reuters was very often on the periphery – projects like Globex or major subsidiaries such as TIBCO and Instinet – rather than on the core business of the information products. So many things got bolted on that no one had a clear view of how they all related to each other.

Job's comments on the Internet were frequently dotted with colourful and slightly odd metaphors. "There are no visionary statements about the multimedia future from Job," Katherine Campbell wrote after interviewing him for the *Financial Times* in 1994. "No platitudes from a man who distrusts management jargon. 'We see through a glass darkly,' he says. 'We are loath to commit ourselves to a grand strategy.' It is rather a case of 'keeping the quiver full of arrows' and expanding in an 'opportunistic way – if that doesn't sound too derogatory'." The interview was headlined 'Presiding over Creative Chaos'.

It was only towards the very end of his time that Job came up with an articulated strategy – that Reuters was to become an Internet company – but by then it was too late. The dotcom bubble was already bursting.

Nobody could fault his passion for Reuters – if you cut him open you would find Reuters written all over the inside, one colleague says. He worked long hours and often right through weekends and, as a result, had an enormous grasp of the details of the business, right down to departmental and country level. He would even spend time on customer helpdesks.

But many, with hindsight, say that this was also a great weakness. He was too close to the detail, and never shook off that journalist's desire to finish one story and get on with the next, to solve a problem and then move on. He had a niggling, obsessive sense of detail and would rarely let a piece of paper pass his desk without wanting to rewrite it. One former director says Job had a 'butterfly mentality'. Like his favourite echidna, his mind kept darting from one thing to another. It never seemed to stay focused long enough to enable him to develop into a strategic thinker.

He could also be mulishly stubborn.

"Peter's biggest problem is that, in his view, in any exchange of views there can be only one person who's right," says former UKI Managing Director John Lowe. "And his initials are probably P followed by J."

"He understood the culture, he was very hard working – too hard working. He was extremely shrewd, numerate, and a great driver of people, but not necessarily the greatest judge of whether to drive them in one particular direction or another.

His major bad point was that he viewed any argument as a contest of wills, and there was only one will that was going to prevail. And that had the obvious effect that eventually people stopped arguing with him. It was career threatening."

One of Job's senior technical and marketing managers also agrees that he had an impressive understanding of the business, product line and customers.

"He was not a technologist and that ultimately may have been his Achilles' heel," he says. "He took what he was given from the product development divisions, and what he was given was never good enough and never arrived quickly enough. He never sorted that out. His fundamental failure was to get to grips with this morass of thousands and thousands of people developing bits of code and databases all over the world and getting in each others' way and not producing coherent quality on time.

"I don't think Peter ever got on top of the enormous multi-headed beast, the hydra that was Reuters core development."

How good was he at judging people? He tended at the outset to surround himself with his former Asian colleagues – it was seen as a 'mafia' by those left outside – but many of the inner circle ultimately let him down. Several of his senior appointments did not survive long in their jobs. Many former colleagues point to what they describe as Job's bullying manner and in particular the way he conducted the monthly executive committee meetings, a dysfunctional and at times quarrelsome group.

"The way he kept tabs on business was bizarre," another

marketing executive recalls. "I used to appear every month at one of these EXE meetings, and I and a lot of others could tell you about waiting for hours in the ante-room because the agenda was running over, and then coming on and doing your twenty-minute spot. Job would completely dominate proceedings from the table but without any decisions ever being taken. It was never clear to me what the purpose of that committee was. Was it an information meeting, some kind of review meeting, or was it a decision-making meeting? It seemed to me to be none of those things, and the agendas always struck me as being the most extraordinary hotch-potch of unrelated matters – things that happened to be Job's flavour of the month. In all the times I was there, I never really participated in any serious discussion or I never heard any serious discussion around the table."

One of the few non-journalists who sat on the committee for several years in the 1990s likened it to a Monty Python sketch.

"It was a gruesome way to manage."

"Basically we were there to listen to Job," he says. "He ran it. The meeting would often open with him and Parcell and Ure quipping in Latin jokes. We sat all day in front of a parade of poor devils who were dragged in to present their business plans. Most left dreadfully bruised. It was a gruesome way to manage."

Another former member said it became increasingly hard to criticize Job.

"Shall we tell the president? There was a terrible sense of not being allowed to criticize, which was totally different from the style he had adopted in Asia. In Asia we were brutally argumentative and tough on each other. He argued with us, we argued with him. But he just lost that in the final years of his reign. It became impossible to propose, or criticize.'

"The executive committee was a toothless tiger. Job increasingly made the decisions with the non-execs, then he changed the structure and we had that Strategy Review Committee, which was just nonsense. Towards the end he was making the decisions on his own."

Job's lack of vision was a 'fundamental tragedy', he adds. "There was no strategy, no vision. If you think about the first five years of Peter's reign it was about running the company better, it was about cutting costs and making people a bit more efficient. But the second five years was seemingly about getting Peter to retire on his sixtieth birthday without having made any major fuck-ups. That's a bit brutal but it's the truth.

"There were plenty of other things we could have done. I used to say that if Renfrew were still running the company, Reuters would have bought Yahoo! when it was much smaller. We would not just have celebrated the fact that we had invested a million dollars and made $40m, we would have bought the whole damned thing. Now you might say now, after the dotcom collapse, that would not have been such a great plan. But it would have made sense, it would have re-positioned Reuters."

A former Asian colleague says there were two Jobs: the entrepreneur in Asia, who pioneered satellite delivery, created local language services and ran an exciting, motivated, innovative and profitable business; and the bureaucrat in London who simply got bogged down in the detail. Perhaps there was also a third, slightly unsure Job, after the FBI investigation.

"Peter changed so much from the time I knew him in Asia

to the time he left as CEO," he says. "His great strengths were in those far flung areas where he could start a business and really crank it up. The detail he got involved with as CEO is staggering. In the end of the day the problem was probably not getting people around him to delegate and really trust, and I don't think he ever really got that.

"Then the business model changed abruptly and there was no strategy for dealing with it."

Job could also bully colleagues in public. He famously put down one of his most senior women executives, Marion King, during a meeting of the company's top 100 managers in Geneva. King, who was at the time running part of Job's former Asian empire, had made a presentation on behalf of a group that had been evaluating a product line in which she had previously been involved. In front of all her peers, Job cut her to pieces in his feedback and never explained to her why he had done so.

It was at the same meeting that a departing executive director criticized some of his board colleagues for regarding ordinary people as 'pond-life' and Job himself for his 'do as I say, not as I do' philosophy.

"There was a huge comfort zone issue with the rich men at the top no longer wanting to mix with the common folk of the company."

"There was a huge comfort zone issue with the rich men at the top no longer wanting to mix with the common folk of the company," one of the top 100 managers at that meeting recalls. "They lost contact. To get a senior director to host something, or to walk the streets with you, was impossible. There was a lack of ambition, lack of hunger and lack of experience of bad times. We had a home-grown group, quite wealthy and pretty arrogant."

Echidna-like, Job spent much of his time as CEO darting around the world. He used to claim that he was the most travelled CEO in Britain – possibly even in the world. His managers in the field were always impressed with his knowledge of the business in their countries, and with his ability to communicate with their customers.

But when back in England, Job seemed to retreat into the past. He oversaw the refurbishment of the 1930s Lutyens-designed head office at 85 Fleet Street, where senior management were closed off in wood-panelled offices on the seventh floor. He turned the top, eighth floor into executive dining rooms and an art gallery for which, from 1992 onwards, he started to collect paintings – mostly eighteenth century and traditional and not at all in keeping with the image of a dynamic modern company.

"I've never cared for anything much – music or theatre – that was written after 1830," he told broadcaster and theatre critic Sheridan Morley in an interview in which he talked about his passion for Schubert and revealed that Shakespeare's *Macbeth* was his favourite play. He had acted in the role of Lady Macbeth at prep school.

He bought a country estate in Oxfordshire and took up shooting. He loved to play the country squire. One couple invited to dinner at his home described it as "slightly less grand than Blenheim Palace".

In the end he cut a lonely figure. A colleague recalls seeing

him at the Chelsea Flower Show – he liked gardening and culti-
vating roses. "You would have expected him to be out there
networking and talking to people," the colleague recalls. "But
instead he was there, notebook in hand, with his nose in each
bloom working out which one to buy for his garden."

"He suffered from deafness in one ear," says one of his former country managers, "and this became more pronounced as
his reign continued."

A POVERTY OF AMBITION

Job inherited a company run on geographical lines; he himself
had emerged from a territorial power base in Asia. For his first
eight years he did little more than tinker with this structure.
The Middle East and Africa were merged with Continental
Europe and front line business units replaced or swallowed up
some smaller countries. This meant the business continued to
run in a fragmented way, a collection of baronial fiefdoms with
different internal management systems and a whole variety of
communications platforms driving local market services. It was
virtually impossible to measure the true profitability of Reuters
products – of which there were now several hundred.

As the clock started ticking down on the 1990s, it became
increasingly clear that the primary driver of Reuters success in
the previous decade – the foreign exchange market – was beginning to falter. The company was over-dependent on the this
market. Several senior managers, including Krishna Biltoo, who
was in charge of Money Products, had warned that the golden
goose was running out of eggs. Analysts and journalists had also

questioned how much longer, with decreasing margins and the coming of the euro, the forex party would last. No one seemed to take much notice until one particular consultant, Craig Heimark, was brought in to look at the business from bottom up.

Heimark was by no means the first consultant to be called into Reuters, nor was he the first to deliver a wake-up call over dependency on foreign exchange, but his analysis appears to have been the first that was taken seriously and virtually the first to be acted on – at least in part. A Brown University graduate and one-time Chicago trader, Heimark was a former head of strategy for SBC Warburg. He looked the part. He was trim, with spectacles, and spoke with a soft, authoritative voice.

He had first looked at Reuters while at Warburg in 1996 and 1997, and had rapidly reached the conclusion that its near-monopoly in foreign exchange was going to run dry and that there was no future in organic growth. This was to be a recurring theme over the next few years. Heimark recommended the company buy State Street Bank – a bold move that would have dramatically transformed and broadened Reuters business base in the US. Boston-based State Street Bank was the primary clearing house for the US securities industry.

But with this proposal Heimark ran into another structural weakness inside Reuters. The company had such successful business models in foreign exchange and dealing that it was incapable of evaluating other business opportunities other than by the foreign exchange matrix. Forgetting that its original business model had been to a large extent a lucky strike, Reuters was always looking for the next FX, the next lottery ticket. It had what Heimark believed was an FX fixation.

But even though the company did not take up Heimark's proposal – indeed under Job it consistently shied away from major strategic purchases – he had made sufficient impression to be invited back a year later to undertake a major analysis of the business. He was by now an independent consultant working at The Hawthorne Group.

The Hawthorne Group reverse engineered what Reuters was saying in public, and quantified that in revenue terms, to show that there was a gaping hole in the budget and that the budget gap was going to get bigger. There were two obvious danger signs ahead: the advent of the euro, which would kill off a huge chunk of the foreign exchange business; and, equally alarming, the declining margins of its customers' foreign exchange business. This was one of his key arguments. The company seemed to be content to ensure that its own foreign exchange margins were still healthy, but had failed to notice that its clients were making less and less money out of the business.

Heimark and his colleagues pulled all this into a presentation to the board at its annual away day at the Cliveden Hotel in 1998. Their message was that the financial services industry generally would shift from organizing around products to focusing on customer buying behaviour. Only a few global full-service firms would survive and most would become specialty suppliers, with declining profitability. Reuters, they said, had all the characteristics of a classic monopolistic player and its foreign exchange business was going to fall off a cliff. Job said his projections were wrong. Most of the directors thought they were too alarmist.

The Hawthorne Group went further. They later told Hogg much of the senior management team should go. Not, they said, because they had necessarily failed but because the nature of the business had changed. Job had been great at expanding the business and riding the foreign exchange tidal wave and setting up a distributor, geographically-based business. But the time was now right for a new brand of management and a new business model.

Hogg ignored him, but what emerged from Heimark's work was the first major structural change in Reuters since Job had taken over. In September 1998, the company switched from being geographically-based to a product-based approach.

Three years later, in response to a further consultant's report, by Marakon Associates, the structure underwent another major upheaval. In September 2001, just after Job had left, Reuters shifted from being product-based to customer-based – from product-push to customer-pull. Twenty years late, in business management at least, Reuters had finally caught up with where Bloomberg started out.

Both reorganizations were fundamentally flawed in at least one aspect, a former marketing director believes. "It was screamingly obvious to me and many others, in advance on both occasions, that we ended up trying to fit the business around the new organization, rather than the other way around."

The first, in 1999, merged Reuters geographical areas into a Global Sales unit under Marchand, to properly globalize the product line and standardize business processes. But, it also artificially split product responsibility between Information Products and Trading Systems, both highly interdependent and sold to the same customers. Global Sales was expected to split its effort along the same lines.

"It was madness," the ex-marketing director says. "Several of us a level below EXE had warned of the likely outcome, but EXE had decided, and that was it." The first new structure lasted just two years.

The 2001 restructuring focused on Customer Segments. New systems implemented two years earlier were now close to delivering globally coherent data to measure costs and revenues, but on a product basis. What was wanted now, though, was to measure profitability and set management targets by Customer Segment.

As years were wasted trying to get the structure right, money was also squandered. In the eyes of his critics, nothing illustrates more the lack of strategic direction or ambition under Job than the £1.5bn of surplus cash that was handed to shareholders in 1998.

Shareholder value had become the mantra in the 1990s and for a while appeared to be driving the company. Finance director Rob Rowley was the main force behind this, which seemed to sum up Reuters refusal to think big. Only one executive director, Parcell, questioned the wisdom of giving up the principal means with which to make a major strategic purchase. Shareholders seemed happy enough, but the *Financial Times* accused Reuters of an 'embarrassment of riches and a poverty of ambition'.

"Giving all that money back to shareholders was a message to shareholders that we cannot think what to do."

"Giving all that money back to shareholders was a message to shareholders that we cannot think what to do," a former marketing executive says "and a message to staff that we do not trust you."

In the absence of big strategic leaps outside the business, Reuters continued to make dozens of tiny, often unrelated acquisitions, in the hopes that one of them would turn out to be the next big win, and also to buy in expensive outsiders from the markets. The outsiders consistently failed – Wilton took Dealing nowhere in ten years and Drayson never delivered the new money products he was hired to build. Carolyn Chin was recruited from IBM in 1998 for $1m to be chief marketing officer in North America. Her gutsy marketing approach led to an advertisement comparing Reuters to Viagra but she lasted only a few months.

Various attempts were made to advertise and to boost the company's brand through the late 1990s, but nobody in the end could ever quite decide what the company was, and therefore what the message was.

TECH TALK

It was never wholly clear whether Reuters was a technology company, or a company that used technology to deliver its services.

Job, though, seemed to be in no doubt. *Financial Times* Editor Andrew Gowers, himself a former Reuters correspondent, recalls asking him whether Reuters was a technology or content company, or a bit of both. "Technology", Job replied without a moment's hesitation.

The ambiguity started even with the analysts who follow Reuters for their investment houses. Few treat Reuters as a pure technology stock. Most are media specialists, even though traditional media accounts for less than 10% of Reuters business and the company has virtually no advertising revenue – an essential component in monitoring the health of media stocks.

The difficulty of positioning Reuters led to the absurd situation of one analyst tracking the company alongside Sketchley – a dry-cleaning company. The analyst's team had divided service companies by alphabetic order so for no better reasons he followed Reuters and Sketchley.

The push for frontier technology was a legacy from Renfrew's time, and it accelerated under Job – although in a haphazard way, and often with little strategic direction. It began with datafeeds and open systems. Reuters led the way. Reuters understood in the early days that customers needed to switch between information sources, and that desk real estate was at a premium – people could not have more than three screens in front of them.

Reuters seized this as an opportunity for revenue by being the pioneer in switching, enabling customers to view multiple sources on a single screen. This ensured it pride of place. Reuters became the industry standard – sometimes in institutions where otherwise, because Reuters lacked the right content, it would have been marginal.

The process started with the acquisition of Rich and with video switching technology, and took a huge leap forward when

Reuters saw that the future was going digital. With the digital revolution, Reuters became the global standard for delivery of financial information services to the end-user's desk. It became the deliverer of its own and everyone else's data. Huge resources in the company were now being devoted to meeting customer requirements for datafeeds, distribution, analysis and display.

Nothing contrasts more sharply with Bloomberg, who throughout the 1990s retained his clunky old box with a retrieval-based technology that hardly changed. This even created a false sense of security. Reuters, with its open systems and broadcast technology, felt it had an unassailable technical ascendancy over Bloomberg. Indeed the feeling was reinforced by positive feedback from clients' IT departments who disliked Bloomberg's 'closed box' approach.

But Bloomberg never let technology get in the way of his end-user. He concentrated instead on content and a user interface which remained defiantly simple – intuitive, easy and familiar. Bloomberg kept his focus on the traders, the actual users. While Reuters technical solution people were talking to the IT departments, Bloomberg's attractive, young staff – often themselves with a markets background – were out on the trading floors talking to the people who would decide, when the crunch came in the financial meltdown in 2001-2003, which of the two systems they would keep. When the choice came, except at the very high end of the market, it was more often than not Bloomberg rather than Reuters. Riding on the success of its technology and carried financially by technical solution revenues, Reuters throughout the 1990s in effect lost sight of the end-users.

"Reuters never managed to get that close to the users. "Bloomberg has."

"Reuters never managed to get that close to the users," says Sharrock, the former Director of Customer Focus. "Bloomberg has. Bloomberg came from inside, and from day one he was setting up tools for traders like himself, following the market wrinkle by wrinkle and applying the technology to do it. And whether the technology was old, like his old mainframe structure, didn't particularly matter to him. What he wanted was what the guy on the desk needed."

Reuters also lost sight of information content.

"At management meetings very little time was spent on content," says former Nordic business manager Ivan Mulcahy. "It was always on numbers of sales, keystations, revenue forecasts, while in fact most of time should have been spent on content. One of the reasons we did not talk content, certainly in continental Europe, was because none of us really understood content – not in a really detailed market user level."

"Not one senior executive director, not Job, Parcell, Ure, Villeneuve, nor the Chairman, Hogg – ever had a profound knowledge of the markets."

"Not one senior executive director, not Job, Parcell, Ure, Villeneuve, nor the Chairman, Hogg – ever had a profound knowledge of the markets. No one had a markets background."

"The ethos of the company was not about content," says

Mulcahy. "Being 'one of us' was vital, someone who was a skilled general manager, trusted and liked by senior management, but profound market-driven understanding was not at a premium."

"Yes, there was excess reliance on the bank's IT departments," says a former senior marketing executive. "Yes, that did mean that we lost contact with the end-user. Moreover, Reuters was never terribly good at recruiting people that have come from the market with a very powerful understanding of the way the markets behave. It made one or two attempts with Ros Wilton and Barry Drayson.

"They, as individual recruitments, were flawed, but there weren't nearly enough of them and I always felt that Reuters relied too heavily on the gifted amateur to run its marketing operations. Once we had lost contact with the end-user, we lost what little feedback there was to be had from the horse's mouth. We did not have an alternative means to get at that knowledge. So we ended up buying broker data, for example, in an increasingly expensive effort to keep our edge in real time information, Bloomberg being by the mid-1990s so far ahead in other data classes and analytics with many of his developments based on direct feedback from end users and. just as important, often delivered almost overnight."

Reuters transformation into a technology company accelerated in the 1990s under the sway of a senior group of technical managers, in particular Mike Sayers, Greg Meekings and Martin Davids. IT consulting began to account for an increasing slice of revenue. Was this a strategic error? Should Reuters have remained an information company that just used technology?

"We got seduced by technology. Seduced by it and then not able to manage it coherently."

"We got seduced by technology," says the former senior marketing executive. "And we lost sight of the fact that the true value of the company lay in being able to collect, aggregate, package and sell information. Seduced by it and then not able to manage it coherently."

"Not so," says one of the former technical directors. "Surely technology has been part of Reuters since the Baron used the telegraph and then cables? Surely it worked best when there was a blend of innovative marketing with leading edge technology? Each side can dominate for a period, but in the end there must be a balance. The trouble is there wasn't a significant new marketing idea after Dealing 2000 and Globex. So the balance was not there."

At times Reuters became overwhelmed by its own technology. It had grown in such a patchwork manner that a route map through the various systems and communications that supported them looked more like a plate of spaghetti than the London Underground map. In the early 1990s league tables appeared regularly in the press saying which companies were spending most on R&D, and Reuters used to come out consistently at or near the top. But the reality is that nearly all of this was spent on maintaining legacy systems and holding together all the mutually incompatible platforms, rather than doing anything really new. There was one fatal decision on the technology front in the early 1990s, and late in the decade three mammoth programmes drained a lot of technical resources and management attention just as the Internet revolution burst into the information markets.

A 'big miss' was IP (Internet Protocol), a failure that underscored Reuters growing inability to make the right technical decisions. By 1992 it was clear from all the technical journals, and to anyone up to speed with new technology, that there was now a pressing need for the entire Reuters network to offer interactive, two-way links, and that most important of all there was a readily available system to achieve this – IP.

Senior technical staff laid on a landmark demonstration to the executive committee. This showed e-mail, file transfer and a Reuters Terminal updating in real time, using IP while operating on a standard IDN subscriber line and, crucially, without any loss or delay.

"This had never been done before," one of the technical managers involved recalls. "The purpose of the demonstration was to prove that it was feasible to re-engineer IDN to support IP on subscriber lines directly, and to leverage commercially available IP applications like e-mail.

"It was so simple, so elegant and so efficient that they could not understand what they were told and shown – IP on a regular IDN line allowing IP applications to share the line with the proprietary Reuters protocol without a massive software effort," the technical manager recalls. "If we had adopted it, we would have had every Reuters Terminal IP or Internet enabled when the Web revolution happened."

The IP gateway would have enabled Reuters to leverage the range of standard software then flooding onto the market. Reuters could then have rolled out a messaging service to rival one of the drivers behind Bloomberg's mounting success. More importantly, it would have connected all Reuters users with each other, enabling Reuters to offer Dealing-like services across all the financial markets. But despite vigorous support from IDN's creator Richard Willis and other senior technical managers, the proposal was turned down – largely because top management could not see a business justification. The IDN concentrator was eventually re-engineered to support IP but it was deployed slowly, and was a very clumsy solution that was neither efficient nor simple.

"Where would Reuters have been today if hundreds of thousands of our terminals had been Internet-ready when the World Wide Web swept around the globe in the mid-1990s?"

"Where would Reuters have been today if hundreds of thousands of our terminals had been Internet-ready when the World Wide Web swept around the globe in the mid-1990s?" asks the technical manager.

Other problems on the technical front were unavoidable. The roll-out of the euro in 1999 and the approach of the millennium, combined with a decision to close down the original Monitor network, concentrated just about every technical resource in the company for several crucial but ultimately wasted years. All the company's services, both domestic and international, had to be primed to handle new currency sets for the euro and then made millennium compliant. At the same time, old services that were still feeding off the original Monitor network had to be shut down or re-engineered. All three projects were costly and a huge distraction.

"What in the end was Reuters core business? Was it information, financial markets, trading rooms, or news? No one ever seemed to know."

"What in the end was Reuters core business?" asks one former business manager. "Was it information, financial markets, trading rooms, or news? No one ever seemed to know. It's an easy throw-away statement: stick to your knitting. I think that has been the downfall of Reuters because when the trading rooms go down, Reuters has nowhere else to go. The tail ended up wagging the dog. The IT function ended up designing products for the company and there was no comprehensive IT strategy. Reuters just wasn't very brave. There was no vision. Reuters had no ambition because it felt it was at the top."

Or was it – others ask – that there were no marketing ideas?

7

Searching for Strategy

One unscripted sentence during a teleconference briefing for analysts and journalists on 21 October 1999 finally exposed the weakness of Job's 'echidna' position on strategy. Asked about the Internet, he said it was "hard to be clear about strategy because there are so many changes in our markets at the moment".

"It was hard to be clear about strategy because there are so many changes in our markets at the moment."

Job said later that of course he had a strategy, and his off-the-cuff remark had been incorrectly interpreted as implying Reuters did not have one. Characteristically, he blamed the misunderstanding on the fact that journalists had been invited to listen in to the briefing and that they had got it all wrong. But the market disagreed and Reuters ever-volatile share price, already badly battered by fears over Instinet following an equally accident-prone analysts' briefing the previous month, slumped to its year's low at £5.17.

It was no coincidence that at about this time the board had started to pay more attention to strategy. Largely at Hogg's insistence, a Strategic Planning Group was set up in late 1998, and although it was put in charge of a home-grown manager, head hunters also started searching for an external candidate to lead it. Inside the company, meanwhile, the Internet pressure was building and those who were calling aggressively for an Internet-based future were finally being heard.

By late 1999 it was obvious that the public Internet would get to the point where it could deliver good enough performance to the vast majority of clients for whom real time was not absolutely critical. They would live with five or ten second delays in prices. Very few needed instantaneous delivery – perhaps fewer than 10% of Reuters clients. In other words there was now a real danger of disintermediation. Exchanges could deliver their data direct to clients and cut out vendors such as Reuters. Few exchanges, though, had yet challenged that proposition and taken on board all the internal plumbing and external management of their data which vendors like Reuters looked after for them. But of more immediate concern, new aggregators of data could spring up to deliver coherent feeds of multi-source information over the Internet at costs far below those of Reuters.

The Strategic Planning Group viewed the Internet as a mortal threat to Reuters core Information Products. But they could not bring the person in charge of those products to see it that way. Parcell remained stubbornly agnostic about the Internet. It simply did not figure in his five-year plan.

"I think he completely misread the Internet revolution," a former colleague says. "Parcell just failed to see that it could cannibalize any revenue at all. I remember at one meeting there was a heated discussion about what would happen if just the lowest 10% of Reuters revenues were lost to the Internet and he could not see it at all and, of course, that is what subsequently happened."

Some who worked under Parcell found him almost impossible to stand up to. "He was a very frightening man, a chain smoker who just stared at you with those dead eyes."

Faced with this obstinacy, the Strategic Planning Group assumed its unofficial role as a secret service and plotted to get rid of Parcell. They prepared some questions for Job to ask him about how Reuters was going to rise to the challenge from competitors better placed to exploit the low cost of entry. Parcell responded by saying he did not believe in the threat. That was virtually the end of his career. His way to the top was blocked by his refusal to budge over the Internet and he resigned in January 2000. Job had by now come round to believing – or being pressured into saying – that Reuters future lay with the Internet. Parcell had not.

The future arrived with a blast in February 2000 when Job announced that Reuters was to become a full Internet company. Up to £500m would be spent over the next four years to switch Reuters information business to an IP-based e-commerce model. Job said the Internet had reached the point where services could be delivered to a market of 60 million semi-professional retail investors for up to $100 a month.

"The Internet is changing dramatically the landscape of Reuters customer base," Job said. "Reuters is no longer about the hundreds of thousands but about the tens of millions, in customer terms. The Internet just opens up a whole new door for us."

The market, still in the grips of the dotcom euphoria, responded with wild enthusiasm and the share price shot up 40% in a week and the following month touched an intra-day high of £17.15. Suddenly Job, who had been pilloried only months before, was greeted as a new hero of the Internet Age. He was applauded at a staff meeting and for one very good reason – most employees were now on paper some £21,000 richer. Under a millennium incentive plan introduced in 1998, all full-time staff who stayed through to September 2001 were granted options on 2,000 shares at £5.50 a share. At the share's highest ever close in London – £16.17 on 7 March 2000 – the potential profit from the millennium options was £21,340.

Even hard-nosed London analysts gave Job a small ovation at the announcement meeting. The tabloid *Daily Mirror*, which months before had berated Job's performance, saying it had sent him a P45 – a tax form given to sacked employees – gracefully withdrew its demands for his resignation.

The wholesale conversion to the Internet was to be underpinned by what came to be called the Gazelle programme and by the technology panned from Reuters already successful investments in Internet start-up companies – the Greenhouse Fund. They would both turn out to be largely empty promises.

The strategy was supported by a brand advertising campaign emphasizing Reuters as a go-ahead, innovative organization that was a natural for the Internet. As part of the pitch to take the message to upscale consumers, Reuters entered its first major sports sponsorship, sponsoring the BMW Williams team in Formula One.

GLOCER'S GAZELLE

Gazelle, like the moonshot-inspired Armstrong, was another programme that was going to be a giant step forward for Reuters. It meant the Web enablement of every aspect of its operations. Gazelle would wean Reuters away from its out-moded delivery networks and migrate almost all its financial services onto the Web through a new communications partner, Radianz.

The objective was to slash delivery fixed costs by two-thirds. This meant replacing IDN. Everyone agreed IDN had been brilliant, had kept Reuters going for fifteen years and was the best of breed. But by the late 1990s it had become hugely expensive compared with the IP alternatives. Radianz was to provide the Web hosting and connectivity that would displace IDN, and all of Reuters technical operations would be out-sourced to Radianz as well as the management of communications.

Glocer, a leading Internet protagonist who had now taken over Information Products from Parcell, was put in charge. Gazelle was his ticket for the top job – and he outlined his vision for it in a strategy paper saying that it would be the group's 'giant leap forward' that would 'change the way we work'.

"All areas of our organization in every part of the world will be affected," he said. "It is the single most important project we have ever undertaken."

Yet by the time Glocer took over formally in June 2001 the programme was already failing. What went wrong? Essentially it suffered from the same problems as Armstrong. It was a massive, technology-led programme which was flawed and never succeeded in winning many customers.

"The idea was to replace IDN with Web hosting," says one technical manager who worked on the project. "But the scale of it all was just too overwhelming. IDN had 400,000 access points. It was not so much the number of instruments as the huge throughput. They simply could not get Gazelle to work. Every time they tried to do something to get round IDN the company failed."

"It was hugely over-hyped by people who had absolutely no idea how the systems they were trying to replace actually worked."

"It was hugely over-hyped by people who had absolutely no idea how the systems they were trying to replace actually worked and, as in all such situations, the spinners eventually came to believe their spin."

At one stage there were ninety people working in the e-commerce platform group – all trying to integrate three off-the-shelf solutions to work together.

Unlike Bloomberg, which just sells one box on which the

client gets everything, Reuters had traditionally sliced and layered its products so that permissioning – enabling a client to see only the data he has paid for – was a major technical issue.

It was also a major technical challenge. At the time of Gazelle, every second Reuters proprietary system was sending out one million quotes in real time on 165,000 equities, 541,000 bonds and over 150,000 derivative products from 263 exchanges in nearly 100 countries. In addition, the system was then storing 2.4m equity research reports covering 28,000 companies and nearly one million news stories generated out of 181 bureaux.

Ambitious 100-day targets were set for developing and launching a series of Web-based products, but far from getting on top of this massive stream of data and news, Gazelle was ultimately overwhelmed by it.

In the end the programme just became an overblown technical project – £500m spent building an e-commerce platform, probably using the wrong open system, and without any commerce hanging off the end of it.

"Gazelle's real failure was that there were no new services. It was just a technical project with no customer in sight," a former member of the Strategic Planning Group says. "It was a technology-led revolution which never established mass market products."

"Reuters had shown the way in Continental Europe with the rollout of a low-cost Web product to middle office departments, Reuters Markets Monitor. If the company had slowly built on this model, which proved quite successful, Gazelle might have worked. But instead they took the thumping all-at-once approach. And it failed."

The all-at-once approach was probably Gazelle's Achilles' heel. There were a host of market initiatives, including services for energy, electricity and equities and, in time, one of these could have eventually led the way to a new e-commerce business model. But in the end the timing was wrong, and the company failed to find its new e-markets; it never found the end consumer.

"We were probably too late," says a former marketing manager. "A very significant part of Reuters business in the twenty-first century can and should be delivered into browsers – either via extranet or Internet – and should be administered in a fully electronic online context. When we finally launched Gazelle in February 2000 we failed to produce new products of significant mass appeal to sell via that Internet."

"What the hell was it?"

A former member of the executive committee still wonders what Gazelle really was. "What the hell was it?" he asks. "It was Glocer's pitch for the CEO position and it sounded great but what was in it? It was all 'Webby', about new ways of doing things."

"Gazelle was a monumental failure."

"It's amazing the way the company abandoned what it knew. For all our self-criticism, we did know a lot about how to run projects and how to manage things. This was about just saying all that stuff is wrong, that you just form these teams who operate independently and they don't have to understand what it is they are trying to deliver, what it is they are trying to get to, what customers they are trying to serve. They just do stuff. It really was nonsense. Gazelle was a monumental failure."

A product manager who was involved in Gazelle says it was a scandal. "The presentations promised that everything would change as a result of Gazelle," says the manager. "But all they ever got out were a few piffling products and a handful of sub-scribers. Then, rather like in the old Soviet Union, Gazelle was airbrushed out."

GREENHOUSE GAS

The Greenhouse Fund was a great Reuters success story for a time but without, as yet, a happy ending. An inspired individual led Reuters to invest in a host of Internet companies with a view to feeding the new technology back into Reuters mainstream business.

John Taysom, the pioneer of the fund, maintains that this did indeed happen and is continuing to happen, but not every-one agrees. Some see the Greenhouse Fund as little more than a mirage and another lost opportunity as no big business or major new initiatives sprang from it and the returns have so far been little more than average.

Taysom had joined Reuters from Price Waterhouse in 1982 just as Monitor was taking off. "I was interviewed by Peter Job and I told him I wanted to be a journalist," says Taysom. "Job said he had just stopped being a journalist and that the company needed commercial managers.

"As an auditor, one of my clients at Price Waterhouse was Beechams. They had just become able to consolidate their cash

balances from overseas operations daily and had begun to subscribe to Reuters Monitor to put them on a par with the banks
acting for them in the wholesale forex market. They were one of
the first corporate treasury departments to take Reuters Monitor. This looked interesting because it would mean a potentially
much larger market for Reuters than just their traditional
market so I decided to jump on the wagon. That was what convinced me to join Reuters, the potential for a broader audience
for their products."

Taysom was posted to Bahrain the following year and it was
in the Middle East, then administratively part of Job's Hong
Kong-based Asian empire, that he began to take an interest in
the underlying technology. "We had sold Reuters into all eleven
banks in Saudi Arabia and the market was saturated so we had to
provide extra features for them in order to gain more revenue.
Because we were an outpost we could not rely on London to
focus on our product needs, that required us to be technically
innovative or wait in line," he says. After sending himself on
numerous day-release courses on networking and databases,
Taysom became technically savvy.

He moved to Silicon Valley in 1994, reporting into the New
York NewMedia group, just after Reuters had purchased
Teknekron in Palo Alto. Teknekron supplied information management systems for trading rooms and Taysom's brief was to
help exploit its natural synergies with Reuters and look out for
the next synergy, for 'tomorrow's technology', before Reuters
even knew it needed it, and before competitors got hold of it.
One result of this was Taysom's proposal to the Teknekron
CEO to spin out a subsidiary, TIBCO Software, to deliver

products to markets outside finance, leaving the finance customer relationships behind in TIBCO Finance.

Taysom's first experience of driving a major external investment himself – Yahoo! – was to prove a turning point. He negotiated to invest in the second-round financing for Yahoo!, offering the Internet start-up an international brand and Reuters news, rates and Teknekron's scaleable internet software. But, frustratingly, taking a stake in Yahoo! required no less than fourteen signatures from Reuters – corporate, North American management and NewMedia.

"By the time we had been round the houses and collected authorization for a $4m stake there was only $1m left because the other three had already been snatched up."

"By the time we had been round the houses and collected authorization for a $4m stake there was only $1m left because the other three had already been snatched up," says Taysom. "The whole point of the Greenhouse Fund was to streamline the decision-making process, make it faster and most importantly to separate the procurement from the fledgling company, where they would be obliged to demonstrate full global support to win Reuters core business, from the investment decision."

The Reuters mergers and acquisition process was aimed at buying 100% of a company. So following the Yahoo! experience, a streamlined process and structure was put in place – 'the Greenhouse Charter' – to enable Reuters Greenhouse to take minority stakes without deploying an army of signatories and act like a normal venture capitalist. The fund's first investment was made in 1995.

Then, in a remarkable display of one half of Reuters not knowing what the other half was doing, Taysom was fired by NewMedia in New York and rapidly re-hired twenty-four hours later by London. Once over that glitch, Taysom went on over the next seven years to put together an impressive suite of investments in start-up Internet technology companies in the US, Europe and Israel. At its peak it had minority investments in eighty-two companies. On the back of the first ten initial public offerings (IPOs) from the fund, when a flotation of the fund itself was mooted at the height of the dotcom boom, brokers said it was worth $1.5bn.

"I never understood on what basis they reached that figure," says Taysom. "It certainly did not come from us. As managers hoping for an IPO it was if anything in our interests to play down the possible value of the fund."

Taysom and the team he built around him when he relocated to London in 1997 made the initial investment decisions virtually autonomously, but the decision to sell was not his alone. That rested with finance director Rob Rowley and it was never clear what his goal was. Some senior managers said it ended up just being a fund into which he tapped when he needed to top-up Treasury.

"We were free to make investments on the way in – we only had one vetoed and that was very early on back in 1995 or 1996 – but Reuters always owned the underlying assets," says Taysom. "When the companies went public we in effect distributed back stock to Reuters – sixteen went IPO and eighteen in addition were sold privately. When it came to sell public stock we might recommend sales, but other factors were in play and ultimately the stock was owned by Reuters Corporate Treasury. In particular, during the period we were slated to go public, the brokers advising Reuters were recommending that we keep a large portfolio of public stock in the fund."

The roll call of investments was impressive, and many have grown into significant stand-alone companies or have been acquired by major corporations: Yahoo!, Digimarc, Infoseek, VeriSign, SpeechWorks – and the profits they made on sale started generating significant profits and cash for Reuters. Almost 10% of first-half profits in 1999 came from sales of stock held by Reuters in companies that had completed successful IPOs, and by the first half of 2000 the Greenhouse Fund was generating 17% of Reuters total operating profit. The company got $70m back just from Yahoo!

The dotcom crash brought the IPO prospects for the Greenhouse Fund back down to earth and Reuters has yet to recoup its original investments, which totalled $400m. The return to date to Reuters in pure cash stands at $370m. But the company retains minority investments in some twenty private companies that have yet to be sold. Several are cash positive and, says Taysom, are showing 'significant potential'.

Taysom believes, and has consistently argued, that the Greenhouse was not only about making money, it was about flowing technology back into the company via a self-funding investment programme. "If you do it the other way round you end up supporting pet corporate projects that are never able to be viable as stand-alone businesses and that no one wants to kill," Taysom says. "Innovation happens in small companies and to understand and harness the impact of Internet technology on products rather than internal company business processes is the business challenge of the decade for many sectors of the economy."

He says almost 40% of the investments they made have achieved a direct product relationship with Reuters. But some senior managers who watched the process question how much this really benefited Reuters.

"This is infinitely higher than any other significant corporate venturing programme we are aware of," Taysom says. "We were investing in things that were basically not dotcoms but formed the technology infrastructure to make commerce and content management work. It was a financially and technologically successful venture and it was a major factor in the cultural change in Reuters that allowed the company to go from having a seasoned British ex-journalist as its head to a technically savvy 42-year-old American deal lawyer as CEO. The reason the company can now shed 3,500 jobs is because it has completely changed the way it works, the way it develops and uses technology."

While the Greenhouse Fund is indeed credited with helping to shift Reuters towards an Internet culture, it was not the only factor at work. And while many of its small investments fed back into significant features and some key projects, there was no single overwhelming investment which transformed the core business or generated large new revenue streams.

Ironically, one of the remaining investments in the fund is in www.forbes.com, which in terms of unique users is the number one Web-based business site in the world. Wasn't that supposed to be where Reuters was going?

"There was a belief that by making small investments in these companies, the technology would come through to the mainstream," a former product manager says, "But that never happened. There was never any major transfer of technology."

THINKING THE UNTHINKABLE

Reuters established a Strategic Planning Group in 1998 – a full fourteen years after it had floated as a public company, and eight years after Job had become CEO. The group was set up at the same time as the company switched from geographical to product management structure with a remit to "think the unthinkable" and with a reporting line to Villeneuve. The choice of Villeneuve was curious. He had been an executive director for almost as long as anyone could remember, but no one had ever accused him of being a strategic thinker.

"In addition to helping the company move towards tighter and more coherent management of resources, the group will also be responsible for out-of-the-box thinking," one of its new directors, Martin Davis, said. "We will identify and research business opportunities that fall outside our currently defined product areas. Nothing in our remit will be unthinkable – nothing will be beyond questioning."

"The non-execs had come to realize that the company lacked strategic direction and the business was being conducted on a short-term basis."

"The group was set up by Hogg because the non-execs had come to realize that the company lacked strategic direction and

163

the business was being conducted on a short-term basis," says a former executive. "Until then there had been no planning, no strategic thinking about the business environment, or about Bloomberg. But in the end it was a sham. Ure and Job were essentially doing the strategic thinking. They did what they wanted even when they had Rupert Barclay."

The story of Rupert Barclay is the story of Reuters attempts to get on top of strategy in the closing years of Job's reign. Barclay, who had been director of group strategy at drinks and fast food group Allied Domecq, was introduced to Reuters by Hogg and hired by Villeneuve. He joined the company as director of group strategy and development in January 2000 and quit under Glocer in November 2001.

Barclay realized soon after arriving at Reuters that he had made a mistake – there was already somebody in charge of strategy. He had joined on condition that he reported directly to Job, but only after settling into his office did he learn that Ure, who had by now stepped down from the board, had the title of strategic adviser to the board. Throughout his stay at Reuters, Barclay had to contend with blurred reporting lines at the top. He came to regard Ure as the *eminence grise*.

Barclay started at Reuters just as top management was putting the final touches to the 8 February Internet presentation in which Job outlined his dotcom vision for Reuters. It was quickly evident to him that there was a sense at the very top of the company that things weren't quite going to plan – in large part because there wasn't a plan.

Reuters, which had in the past prided itself on not using consultants, was by now awash with them. Booz-Allen &

Hamilton and Marakon Associates were working flat out on various projects. Barclay developed strong views early on and concluded that Reuters had no future in growing its business organically. The company had two and a half monopolies – Dealing, Triarch and a duopoly with Bloomberg in the terminals market – and the problem, he concluded, about being a monopoly is that people will not pay for improvements. So Reuters was condemned to running fast just to stand still.

Barclay decided Reuters had to buy itself out of trouble before the bubble burst. People working with him said he was quickly aware that the soaring share price had more to do with the valuation of TIBCO, in which Reuters was the major shareholder, than with the market's faith in the long-term growth prospects of its core business. TIBCO's market capitalization had risen to close to $30bn in April 2000 from just $1bn the previous year.

Barclay was afraid that Reuters high share price was masking, and therefore putting off, the fundamental and uncomfortable questions about the core business. But he also saw the high market valuation as a 'once-in-a-lifetime' opportunity that had to be seized quickly and boldly.

He outlined his concerns to board members at the 2000 away-day at a country hotel. His presentation posed challenging questions about the post-bubble world he saw coming. Barclay warned that the core business was running out of steam, and said the company had to move into new markets. Reuters must leverage its balance sheet, he argued, and exploit the current high share price to issue paper and make a major strategic acquisition. Aware of the successful acquisition trails of companies like Reed Elsevier and Thomson, whose Thomson Financial unit was now moving up the value chain to challenge Reuters, he proposed SunGard Data Systems as a potential target.

Rowley, who had been receiving advice from a UK strategy consultancy LEK on a host of possible acquisitions for several years, seemed receptive to Barclay's analysis, but Job found it very difficult to accept a plan predicated on a decline in Dealing and other core financial service product revenues. He seemed to argue that if you formulate a plan based on the premise that something will fall off a cliff, then it will fall. Job was in effect responding to Barclay in much the same way that he had dismissed Craig Heimark several years earlier.

Nothing came of Barclay's strategy proposals, and he increasingly devoted his time to leading the Reuters team that floated Instinet in May 2001.

SPACE WALKING

Reuterspace was like the last throw of the dice. Originally set up as Reuters Ventures under Jeremy Penn at the end of 1999, the division was given a new name and a new boss a few months later, at the same time as Reuters announced its Internet future in February 2000. Everything that was not core financial business was thrown into Reuterspace, including traditional and new media, television, business-to-business, retail finance, wireless markets and the Greenhouse Fund. Rowley relinquished his role as finance director to take charge of it, in what many saw as his bid to prove himself as a top-flight businessman and lay down his marker for the top job.

"The finance director is there to protect the money bags, and the Reuterspace chief executive is out there to take risks . . . to make Internet moves without at the moment knowing exactly what the return will be," Job told Reuters Television at the time of the appointment.

Reuterspace suddenly seemed to be an exciting place to be and a lot of the company's brightest young executives clamoured to join – encouraged by the big swank offices in New York and hugely inflated salaries. Executives were transferred from London to New York, in some cases on double the salary.

The objective was to do new things in new ways and hundreds of millions were poured into Reuterspace. People who worked there described it as a chaos of new ideas. It quickly became apparent that Penn was the driving force. Rowley did not develop a track record for taking things forward dynamically.

Following Barclay's lead, Penn came up with two bold proposals for strategic purchases. The first was a multi-billion dollar deal to buy Dun & Bradstreet. This would have given Reuters one of the best-known business information names in the US, and one of the world's top rating agencies, Moody's, which was still then owned by D&B. This was thinking big, but Job again said no. Penn's next proposal was to buy Gartner, the technology research company. This time Hogg said no, and even blocked discussion of it at the board.

One of the senior Reuterspace executives at the time says in the end there was no buy-in to taking the company into new areas. "The moment technology stocks started to fall away in April 2000 the board more or less breathed a sigh of relief and said: 'Thank God for that, we don't have to worry about that any more'. That's when we started to propose things like D&B and Gartner but it needed a strategy, a leap of faith."

"Here was a chance to get into the corporate market and to broaden the base. There was no risk-taking, no strategic framework into which to place things. This is what Barclay was trying to get to in the Corporate Strategy Group. We knew that the company needed a game plan, it had to get beyond the financial markets, it needed to use its present balance sheet strengths, its present borrowing power to expand."

Reuterspace also sought to build its own businesses. The most notable was Kalends, a new service targeting a hitherto largely untouched sector of the world's information market – the future. The brainchild of Dean Ratcliffe, Kalends was a listings service designed to tell people what was going to happen in the future. A marketer who had been in charge of marketing London's Millennium Dome, Sholto Douglas-Home, was recruited to promote the product and £12m was spent on it, but eventually funding was cut and the service was folded back into Reuters main editorial operations.

Kalends was one of several projects that for a while formed part of the 'Incubator'. This was a project to nurture home-grown ideas, and a lot of money and many consultant hours were poured into it. Incubation workshops were held and an Incubation board was established – with chief technology officer Mike Sayers, Penn and editor-in-chief Geert Linnebank among its members. About a dozen ideas were incubated, including Kalends (although this was backed into the Incubator to make it look as though there was some planning), a portal and forum for professional economists, and a global trading and information service for seafood. All of these ideas, good matches for Reuters, came to nothing. Kalends was 'Reuterized' – made to adopt Reuters systems and practices – then integrated back into the company, and the others were shut down as part of general budget cuts.

Another Incubator project never made it out of the winner's enclosure. The company sponsored an Incubator competition and a number of people entered. Glocer handed over a cheque to the winner in New York, but the winning entry – a scheme to trade carbon dioxide emission quotas as a hedge against pollution controls – never started and the Incubator was closed down shortly afterwards.

"The Incubator was great in theory. It was set up to stop good ideas and good people leaving the company. But it was the usual story, and Reuters packed it in before it got going."

"The Incubator was great in theory," one participant says. "It was set up to stop good ideas and good people leaving the company. But it was the usual story, and Reuters packed it in before it got going."

A retail strategy came and went with similar despatch. Money was poured into creating a Reuters e-mall but no major business ever flowed through it. A consumer marketer was brought in to pave the way for Reuters push into the retail financial markets that would be opened up by Gazelle. Kevin McCarten, former group marketing director at the UK supermarket group Sainsbury's, lasted just six months. He left as Glocer announced his first round of job cuts and restructured the company along customer lines. "The role I envisaged did not materialize," McCarten said on leaving.

Reuterspace was launched to acquire new business and build new business but in the end, executives say, it did little other than provide a home for the company's existing Greenhouse Fund and media division.

HOGG TIED

Reuters long-time chairman, Sir Christopher Hogg, has admirers and detractors. Most of the former are outside Reuters while the latter are well established inside the company and among its former employees. To the investment and shareholder community, Hogg brought the sweet scent of success and the promise of good corporate governance. Hogg rarely meets analysts, but talks to journalists and is a star performer at public meetings. He handled a hostile audience at the 2003 AGM, where shareholders criticized Glocer's bonus, with tact and firmness. Inside Reuters, in terms of the business, he does not seem to have contributed very much.

"Chris Hogg is an extremely conservative chairman," says a former director who worked closely with him, "If you look at his record, it is one of making companies smaller. He made Courtaulds smaller and then divided it into two. Allied Domecq and Reuters the same. One was constantly up against the view that everything was too difficult, that you had to focus narrowly on the core business, that you could not use the balance sheet strength to expand elsewhere."

"He once said at the board that what Reuters needed to do

was to find acquisitions – either very small or things like Teknekron and Instinet. Well everybody wants to buy Teknekrons and Instinets but there are not many of them out there. The idea that you can multiply your money by a thousand fold every time you make an acquisition is just nonsense. Chris was sort of dreaming."

Hogg stuck to his guns on large acquisitions to the end. At the 2003 AGM, by which time the company had announced that it was looking for his successor, he came close to congratulating himself and the board for not having made any major strategic acquisitions.

"I make no comment on your Marconi parallel," Hogg told a disgruntled shareholder, "It's perfectly obvious that we are in difficult times. But what we have not done is to spend a great deal of the cash that we earned in earlier years on making large acquisitions. In the course of the 1990s we returned something like two and a half times the value of the company at flotation to the shareholders – £2bn of cash."

"Hogg was a slightly irrelevant person," a former key marketing executive says. "He never seems to have understood the business."

"Sir Christopher may have brought good things to Reuters such as a lead in correct corporate governance," says the marketing executive, "but he never understood the business, not even in his later years when he spent several days a week there. He would still ask questions of the utmost naïvety, so clearly his ability to contribute to strategic or operational management decision making was virtually nil."

"I heard Hogg say once that he thought the only responsi-

bility of a chairman was the appointment of a chief executive,"
says another manager who worked under him. "I think he has
got it wrong twice in the Reuters context, and at least once in
the Courtaulds context. He doesn't have a terrific track record."

8

The Yanks are Coming!

Glocer officially took over on Job's sixtieth birthday in July 2001 but had been calling the shots since the previous December. He swept in with another major reorganization and a wave of redundancies which were announced on the eve of the party to celebrate Reuters 150th anniversary.

The new chief executive's preparation for what would turn out to be a complex and demanding job was 'lite'. His academic credentials were impeccable – Columbia College and Yale Law School – and his work for New York law firm Davis Polk & Wardell had given him international experience in both Tokyo and Paris, and possibly a healthy scepticism about acquisitions. As well as mergers and acquisitions, Glocer worked on management buy-outs, venture capital financing and capital market offerings, but frequently repeated that he had seen many acquisitions that did not work. While at Davis Polk & Wardell he wrote simulation software on litigation techniques, but he did not become a partner. There was nothing meteoric in his early career, but once in Reuters, which he had joined as general counsel and executive vice-president for the Americas in 1993, he moved up so rapidly that he was rarely in the same job for more than a year.

He was plunged into the deep end as legal counsel, working through some of the ugly American law suits and cutting his teeth in the early New Media acquisitions. Glocer was part of a ludicrously top-heavy management team – one of seventeen executive vice-presidents reporting to Mike Sanderson. It was Sanderson who gave him his first big break. With unintended insensitivity, he summoned Glocer, who is Jewish, on Yom Kippur, the most sacred day in the Jewish year normally spent fasting and in prayer. Glocer went along and was offered the job as chief executive for Latin America.

"There was a suspicion that someone locally wanted to destroy the permissioning records to cover up some shady deals."

He hit the ground running in South America, starting in October 1996, and showed his mettle, and a touch of ruthlessness, early on by firing Oli Lunder, the Norwegian manager of Reuters Brazil. A few months later, in April 1997, the Reuters office in São Paulo went up in flames. The fire had started in the accounting department just as a new billing and reporting system was being installed. "There was a suspicion that someone locally wanted to destroy the permissioning records to cover up some shady deals," a former Reuters Latin America executive says. Glocer flew down to São Paulo from New York, and rolled up his sleeves to help his chief financial officer Isaac Piha sort out the crisis.

"He worked round the clock and was very fast at making decisions and implementing them," says Piha. "It was like he was racing to catch a train to the next promotion. I think he expected or knew that Latam was a one-year stint from the outset. He had vast energy and was somewhat out of place with the *mañana* pace of Latin America."

Glocer in fact ran Latin America for eighteen months, and during that time pushed Reuters to invest early in several Web companies – Patagon.com in Argentina, Universal Online in Brazil and StarMedia in Mexico. One of his major achievements was to close down the separate Latam management structure in New York and merge it with North American management. The merger, originally proposed by Piha, produced significant cost savings.

Even then Glocer was staking out his claims and was not shy about his e-vision for the future. Asked in December 1997 in an interview with *Reuters World*, the house magazine, what he saw as the major global challenges, he replied: "The Internet – not only in the widely accepted sense of incorporating Web tools into our products and delivery networks but also in adopting the brutally rapid product development and obsolescence cycles now driving the Web's technology curve."

He took over from Sanderson as president of Reuters America in October 1998 and became increasingly bullish about Reuters Internet future. In a feature headlined '.COM CRAZY ABOUT THE FUTURE', Glocer told *Reuters World* in December 1999 the company should be aiming to capitalize on its brand

and reach out to a mass global market. He was now talking in terms of a billion customers.

"I think Reuters future lies in serving very many more customers than we do today," he said. "I have come to question whether our role should be to essentially hide in the background and just to enable a bunch of portals and aggregators, or whether we shouldn't actually build our brand and got straight to the consumer. The ultimate success of the company will be more like a billion customers globally."

In January 2000 Parcell quit Reuters over his disagreement with the Internet vision and Glocer, the great advocate of the e-future, replaced him as head of the company's major revenue earners, Information Products. Glocer remained president of Reuters America, took a seat on the board in June 2000 and became chairman of the group steering Gazelle, which was to be his transition project.

Reuters announced on 6 December 2000 that Glocer, aged forty-one, would replace Job as CEO. Its shares jumped 7% on the news, reaching £12.72 in late London trading. The *Financial Times* said Glocer 'looks an astute choice' and most analysts and commentators saw his appointment as affirmation of Reuters Internet strategy.

"He has a strong knowledge of Internet technology and what that can do for the group," said Andrew Gordon-Brown, then media analyst at JP Morgan. "He is a guy who is comfortable with what it means from a technical perspective to transform this business."

"I suppose you could say that I was one of the founders of Reuters Internet strategy," Glocer told an interviewer in the

Mail on Sunday. "But it would be a mistake to assume that the fate of Reuters now lies in the hands of an Internet 'nerd'."

Amid all the hype and expectation, a Reuters reporter, Mark Bendeich, was one of the few to sound a note a caution.

"His rapid climb in Reuters was accompanied by a long bull market on Wall Street, rapid growth in retail stock trading and a record US economic expansion," Bendeich wrote. "But industry observers say his skills will be tested going forward with a looming bear market, continued bank mergers and a sobering re-evaluation of the Internet's profitability."

In a spate of press interviews after his appointment, Glocer said the Internet strategy remained on course and stressed that Reuters was both an information and technology company. "What makes Reuters strong is a combination of content, technology and connectivity," he told the *Sunday Times*. "I don't think we can lose any one piece."

Just two years later, with the share price crashing below £1, Glocer had indeed lost several of the pieces and he was now talking about Reuters retrenching as just an information company. It had been a tough learning curve, steering through one of the most severe market downturns in decades a company *The Economist* now described as "a bloated, self-satisfied, rather patrician organization that operated more like a branch of the civil service than a leader of the information age". The way Glocer was to hack back staff numbers indicated he was well in tune with this verdict.

The downturn had already set in before he took over and, when Job announced annual results for the last time in February 2001, Reuters had dropped plans to float the Greenhouse Fund.

The Internet bubble had burst and the fund had lost more than 75% of its value. But Job insisted the Internet strategy remained on course. "The collapse of the valuation bubble around Internet stocks has not affected our strategy, which goes forward as stated last year," he said.

REARRANGING DECKCHAIRS

Glocer had started out with a major strategic shift. As part of the plan for the takeover, he had prepared a company reorganization that would be the third major restructuring in five years. By the standards of Reuters North America, which had undergone eleven 're-orgs' in ten years, this was not excessive, but the switch from running the business on a geographical base, which was reshaped in 1996, to a products base in 1999 and then to a customer base in 2001, left both staff and customers confused and caused considerable upheaval. Restructuring and slimming down also came at a price.

Reuters spent over £600m on business transformation and restructuring between 2000 and 2003, with a further £340m planned for the next three years – not far short of £1bn in total. One former member of the executive committee describes the constant reorganizations as a "hugely expensive, hugely divisive distraction," adding: "I can recall when people would speak of nothing but what their role might be in the new scheme of things."

In terms of learning from Bloomberg's success and Reuters recent failures, however, customer-pull, a way forward devised for Reuters by Marakon Associates, seemed the right solution.

As part of the new customer focus, Reuterspace was folded back into the main business – a move widely interpreted as a signal that the e-future was not going quite to plan.

But to many, it seemed the reorganizations were simply an exercise in rearranging the deckchairs on the *Titanic* when Reuters had already been holed below the waterline, not by an iceberg, but by a Bloomberg.

Close associates say that only in the months after he had taken over did it begin to become apparent to Glocer that he had inherited a seriously sick business. Core revenues were starting to suffer, the Internet strategy was failing to deliver and the usual standby – Instinet – was turning from cash cow into a sick dog.

In May 2001 Instinet was floated on the NASDAQ exchange to raise $464m which, together with an acquisition paid for in shares, reduced Reuters shareholding to 83%. The stock-financed purchase of a competitor, Island ECN, the following year reduced it further to 63%. Instinet needed to buy Island because it had fallen behind in the technology race – Island offered a more cost effective and technically better service. Instinet, in its unsuccessful attempts to branch into bonds trading and retail, had taken its eyes off its own core business and had been overtaken by a more nimble competitor. It had been well and truly 'Reuterized'.

Falling US stock market prices and trading volumes midway through 2001 and the nosedive after the 11 September attacks exacerbated Instinet's woes, and it suffered its first loss since Reuters had bought it, plunging $735m into the red. It responded with cuts in staffing and other costs, but revenues slipped further in the first quarter of 2003, though the loss was pared to $34m.

Much of Glocer's attention in his early months as CEO was spent trying to sort out the problems at Instinet and negotiate the Island takeover. Turning his attention to head office, he appears to have concluded early on that he was going have to clean out the old Reuters, ruthlessly and systematically.

He became Reuters chief hatchet-man through both conviction and necessity. Reporting his first set of interim results in July 2001, he said 1,100 jobs would be shed by the end of 2002, though in the wake of 11 September he upped the target to 1,600 in October and 1,800 four months later. Among the first to go was a group of fifty top managers unceremoniously dumped within days of Glocer's taking over.

These included Krishna Biltoo, director of Credit and Risk Business, Heinrich Wenzel, director of Global Accounts, Bob Etherington, a legendary sales executive who had risen to head global sales training, and David Brocklehurst, the managing director for Australia and New Zealand, as well as most of Marchand's senior managers. Parcell loyalists had already been eliminated, but with this latest batch went hundreds of years of experience and knowledge of Reuters markets and customers. At one fell swoop, a large part of the corporate memory was eliminated – almost certainly an intentional move.

"A blame and compliance culture."

In the 1970s and 1980s, even into the early 1990s, Reuters had been a company where a degree of eccentricity was tolerated, even encouraged as a stimulus to creativity. In the latter part of the Job era and under the new regime that had changed, Mark Trasenster, UKI's managing director for Media until 2002 says, characterizing the new ethos as 'a blame and compliance culture'.

Many of the outgoing executives were iconoclasts, not afraid to criticize, or challenge, while remaining deeply loyal to the company. Their warnings about Reuters direction had been ignored, but they were now inescapably seen as pillars of the *ancien régime*. "We were regarded as the Job generation. Therefore we had to go," says Wenzel. "We were in the way of the change in the culture."

By the end of the 2001 there was a totally new top management team in place. Ure had stepped down from the board a year earlier, while remaining its strategic adviser. He might have been expected to follow the rest of the old guard into comfortable retirement, but Glocer says he pressed him to stay on, greatly valuing his 'strategic brilliance'.

Marchand, however, left Reuters in September and Rowley at the end of the year. Glocer brought Geoff Weetman, the head of Human Resources, onto the board, in what was seen as a reward for his cool handling of the various crises in the US – among them the FBI investigation.

Weetman was an accountant who had been Job's deputy MD in Asia and became MD Asia before taking up a senior post in London. He didn't stay on the board long, retiring a year later with a payoff of £600,000 and a £5m pension pot, prompting adverse press comment when details emerged in the 2002 Annual Report.

Newly installed finance director David Grigson had moved

to Reuters only a year earlier from the UK press group EMAP, where he held the same position as well as chairing EMAP Digital, giving him a solid grounding in media and information as well as strong financial credentials.

A less obvious fit was Philip Green, who joined from international courier group DHL, in September 1999 as head of Trading Solutions. He was appointed to the board just six months later and, to the astonishment of many, became Glocer's chief operating officer in July 2001.

He told a gathering of journalists and analysts in Geneva, however, that DHL and Reuters had much in common; they both moved things from one place to another, and had a lot of banks as customers. So that was all right, then. A born-again Christian, Green came to be known among the lower ranks as Pastor Phil for his annoying and intrusive habit of asking colleagues how often they went to church. He led senior colleagues on a character- and team-building climb to the top of Kilimanjaro.

Green also had a colourful past. Prior to DHL, he had been managing director of the British home furnishings group Coloroll, which collapsed in 1990, and a trustee of its directors' retirement benefits scheme. After a complaint by a fellow director relating to purchase by the scheme of the Coloroll chairman's flat, later sold at a loss, and arrangements regarding the chairman's final salary, Green and his fellow trustees were found guilty by the UK's Pensions Ombudsman in 1994 of maladministration and breach of trust.

Rosemary Martin had become company secretary in 1999, after joining in 1997, and Glocer bought fellow American lawyer and close friend Devin Wenig, who joined Reuters in 1993, onto the board in 2003. By this time these five executive directors had a combined service of some thirty-three years, two less than David Ure.

Green's former DHL colleague Marc Duale was brought in to head Reuters Asia, while a more obviously relevant appointment was that of Jane Platt, former chief executive of Barclays Stockbrokers and Barclays Bank Trust, as head of asset management services.

TERROR AND TURMOIL

Glocer's first big test came on 11 September 2001. Six Reuters staff died when the hijacked American airliners slammed into the twin towers of the World Trade Centre. In the emotionally charged atmosphere, American staff draped a huge Stars and Stripes from the windows of Reuters brand new US headquarters on Times Square, opened just a few months earlier by UN Secretary-General Kofi Annan. This understandable display of patriotism threatened Reuters all-important principle of impartiality and was swiftly removed.

But Reuters came under heavy fire from US politicians and media for its refusal to use the word 'terrorist' in its reporting on 11 September and its aftermath. It was a long-standing editorial principle, the word seen by Reuters as emotive and contravening its all-important impartiality. Margaret Thatcher had once described Nelson Mandela as a terrorist. Former Israeli premier Menachim Begin headed the Irgun guerrilla group which fought against British administration of Palestine in the 1940s and ordered the bombing of Jerusalem's King David Hotel, which killed ninety-one. Are such people freedom fighters or terrorists? It depends which side you are on. Reuters was on no one's, and had always used straightforward descriptive nouns such as 'gunman', 'guerrilla' or 'bomber' rather than 'terrorist'.

A leaked internal memo on the issue from head of news Stephen Jukes, however, used the phrase "one man's terrorist is another man's freedom fighter". It provoked a storm of protest, one American media commentator describing Jukes as having "no moral compass". J. C. Watts, chairman of the House Republican Conference, called on Reuters to rescind its ban on the word. "I fail to see how this noun is not an accurate portrayal of the aggressors who committed the acts of violence witnessed by the entire world last month," he said in a letter to Glocer, urging fellow congressmen to bombard Reuters with protests.

"We've taken a lot of heat on this," Jukes told one newspaper columnist with more than a degree of understatement.

Glocer and editor-in-chief Geert Linnebank defended the policy in a joint statement at the beginning of October, but conceded Jukes' memo had "caused deep offence among members of our staff, our readers and the public at large, many of whom felt this meant Reuters was somehow making a value judgment concerning the attacks."

"This was never our intention, nor is it our policy," they said. "Our policy is to avoid the use of emotional terms and not make value judgments concerning the facts we attempt to report accurately and fairly. We apologize for the insensitive manner in

184

which we characterized this policy and we extend our sympathy to all those who have been affected by these tragic events."

These embarrassments aside, the impact of 11 September on Reuters already precarious business was disastrous. Stock markets had been drifting lower for eighteen months, but now went into freefall as a tidal wave of panic swept world markets. American and British troops poured into Afghanistan, and Wall Street dropped by over 20% before the swift defeat of the Taleban restored a measure of confidence. Reuters shares dropped from £6.49 at the London close on 10 September to £5.26 ten days later.

It was always going to be a bad year, but the scale of the downturn in Reuters fortunes took the markets by surprise. Reuters profits had suffered slight dips in 1997 and 1998, but pre-tax profits for 2001 slumped more than 75% to £158m, despite an 8% growth in revenue to £3.9bn. The total dividend for the year was cut to 10 pence a share from 16 pence, the first reduction since Reuters had gone public in 1984. The outlook for 2002, it said, was for a small decline in underlying revenues. The share price had slipped to just under £6.00 over the previous three months, but dropped 40 pence on the news.

The markets drifted quietly into 2002 before a wave of gloomy corporate earnings reports around the world raised the spectre of recession and triggered a more sustained meltdown in stock prices. By the third quarter, Wall Street, London and other major markets were more than a third below the peaks they had scaled around the millennium. Frightened investors were turning to government bonds and deposits, or stuffing their cash under the mattress.

The advent of the euro had already massively reduced trading volume and, consequently, the number of dealers in the foreign exchange markets. Now, as equities plummeted, investment banks and brokers began to shed staff in droves. By the end of 2002 it was estimated that 100,000 jobs in the major financial markets had gone in the previous two years in the most savage bear market in decades. Reuters major clients were no longer making money.

Inevitably, that meant a huge slump in demand for Reuters screens. User numbers, including clients who accessed Reuters on their own terminals through data feeds, had topped half a million in 2000 and hit 592,000 in 2001, helped by the acquisition of former competitor Bridge, which brought in 80,000 new users. But by the end of 2002 the total had dropped to 493,000, falling further to 469,000 by April 2003, down more than 20% in just 18 months, with further declines in prospect.

While Reuters pointed to a 'fundamental change' in its markets, not all of the decline was down to market shrinkage. Reuters was facing increasing competition at the bottom end of the market from rivals such as Canadian-based Thomson Financial and Web-savvy upstarts such as Caplin Systems in the UK, Amsterdam-based MarketXS and Moneyline Telerate with cheap Internet-based offerings, while Bloomberg continued to lure clients away from Reuters over-complex, high-tech terminals higher up the market.

More worryingly, traders who used to have the luxury of both Bloomberg and Reuters were now being routinely asked to choose one or the other as banks pared costs. Whereas in the past they would hang on to Reuters 'come hell or high water', now invariably they kept their Bloombergs. One leading analyst in London said he would regularly take straw polls among dealers and the 'vote' was running at 4–1 in favour of Bloomberg.

Bloomberg had built a better mousetrap, and the world had beaten a path to his door.

Bloomberg's growth had been phenomenal. From its initial base within Merrill Lynch, it took eight years to get 10,000 terminals into the market. By 1995, the number had reached 50,000, topping 100,000 three years later, 150,000 in the millennium and 175,000 by May 2003. Crucially, each Bloomberg terminal was estimated by industry analysts to be earning almost four times the average paid by Reuters users. Bloomberg had built a better mousetrap, and the world had beaten a path to his door.

After watching the Bloomberg numbers rise steadily, first with a measure of indifference, then with a determined counter-attack and finally with a degree of fatalism, Reuters conceded in April 2003 that it had been overtaken. While Reuters had increased its share of the $6.5bn global information market by 2% the previous year to 39%, finance director David Grigson reported, Bloomberg's share had grown 4% to 42%. Both had been hit by the horrendous downturn in the markets, but Bloomberg was better weathering the storm.

GETTING TO GRIPS

Glocer had ridden into town on a wave of optimism. His £500m project Gazelle was going to transform Reuters. Three years on, the company remained largely dependent on top-tier products and cumbersome and costly networks, with only a small range of Internet-based lower-tier products on offer. Its revenue base remained narrow and under serious threat. Reuters, like a supertanker, was taking a long time to turn.

Trapped between his desire to maintain the 'nice guy' image and the business imperative to cut costs, Glocer had perhaps moved too cautiously at the outset. Associates say he had not wanted to be seen as a 'slash and burn merchant', and that only after the markets plunged in the wake of 11 September did he begin to realize the full scale of the problems.

By mid-2002 it was too late for such niceties and alarm bells were starting to ring, both inside and outside Reuters. The *Financial Times* quoted a major shareholder as saying Glocer had inherited a poisoned chalice, but questioning whether there was any substance behind his 'management jargon'. The *Daily Telegraph* went further, saying Glocer "does not help himself by sending his messages from the battle front in consultant jargon and techno-speak".

In July 2002, Glocer announced a first-half pre-tax loss for the group of £88m – significantly below stock market forecasts – on revenues down 5% to £1.8bn. The losses stemmed mainly from Instinet's plunge into the red and from ongoing restructuring costs. Reuters own pre-tax profits were down by nearly 60% at £47m, though revenues were up 5%. "The core Reuters business has performed resiliently," Glocer said, cautioning that market conditions would remain 'challenging'. Now at £3.00, the share price dropped below £2.50 as analysts yet again started revising downwards their profit forecasts for the full year.

In October, Reuters announced amid great fanfare that it was launching a messaging service for the financial markets, developed jointly with Microsoft. It was at least ten years late. Bloomberg had been providing its clients with messaging since 1992. It was one of Bloomberg's 'killer' features and had helped the service achieve widespread acceptance and create a virtual business community. Bloomberg clients used it not only for business messages, but to arrange to meet for a drink or to send each other jokes, all before the advent of widespread e-mail. "I'll Bloomberg you" was part of dealers' everyday language. Reuters sales force had long clamoured for a feature to compete with Bloomberg messaging. Nobody, they knew, ever 'Reutered' anyone.

Reuters failure to come up with its own version earlier is in part the story of its inability to resolve its internal mastery – technical or marketing. The technology was there long before marketing understood the need for it. The conversational Dealing service, after all, was a messaging service, Instinet had a messaging capability and Reuters journalists had been able to send messages to colleagues' editing terminals for years. There was a botched attempt to launch a messaging product in the mid-1990s – Reuter Mail. Both Marketing and Development blamed the other for its failure. By the time the Reuters service was launched - given away to clients as a free add-on to existing services – everyone had for years been using either Bloomberg, which was generating up to two million messages a day, or e-mail. Although Reuters claimed over 200,000 subscribers for the new messaging service, insiders said usage was minimal.

Worst of all, it was on a separate application so users had to log in and out of it.

In November, Merrill Lynch announced it was awarding a contract for 27,000 desktops for its world-wide retail brokerage network to Thomson Financial rather than Reuters. The five-year deal was worth an estimated $1bn. Reuters, Glocer said, was not prepared to lower its prices to buy business, adding: "We have worked very hard to improve our margins in 2002, and even for a valued client like Merrill Lynch we will not compromise this progress." Reuters share price was now below £2.00.

The bombshell came on 18 February 2003. Reuters had suffered a group pre-tax loss for 2002 of nearly £500m.

The bombshell came on 18 February 2003. Reuters had suffered a group pre-tax loss for 2002 of nearly £500m, after 2001's disappointing £158m profit, with revenues actually down 8% to £3.6bn – the first significant drop in over fifty years. Much of the deficit again stemmed from huge losses at Instinet, but Reuters core business suffered an underlying fall of 6% in revenues and a pre-tax loss of £123m.

Glocer responded with a new programme – this time attacking Reuters bloated product line. Reuters would slash its product range to just 200 services from 1,000, and move to a single delivery platform. Dubbed 'Fast Forward', the programme would cost £340m over the next three years, but aimed to generate savings of £440m a year by 2006. At its heart, though, were another 3,000 jobs losses on top of the 3,200 shed over the previous three years. The few surviving cynics in Reuters suggested the programme might more appropriately have been called 'Eject'.

With bad news mounting, Reuters had hired Simon Walker as its new director of corporate communications, reputedly on a package well into six figures. He had previously been at Buckingham Palace as communications secretary to the Queen, so was no stranger to the media microscope. But there was little he could do about the torrent of critical headlines, which made for unpleasant reading at 85 Fleet Street.

"Agent of its own misfortune . . . Is Reuters terminally ill?"

"Agent of its own misfortune," declared the *Guardian*. "Is Reuters terminally ill?" asked *The Economist*. Blaming Reuters two knights, Job and Hogg, for Reuters predicament, it noted that Glocer had struggled to "transform the Reuters culture from stifling bureaucracy to something dynamic, commercial and Bloomberg-like". From £1.65 before the results, the share price had slumped to £1.18 by the end of the month.

Worse was in store. When the annual report came out the following month the media seized on the £612,000 bonus it showed Glocer had received for 2002, despite presiding over a massive loss and a slump in the share price. This was on top of a salary of £816,000 and benefits, including a housing allowance, of £282,000. Not to mention a relocation allowance of £525,000 paid to him in 2001. In the 1970s correspondents moving to far-flung bureaux got a 'tropical kit allowance' of £100. Philip Green had received bonuses and other benefits on top of his £450,000 salary which took his total earnings to £836,000 and

David Grigson's total package was £690,000 while Hogg, as part-time chairman, got £277,000.

Whatever other criticisms might have been levelled at them, Job and his fellow executive directors had rarely been accused of 'fat-cattery'. Job in his last full year had earned just over £1m and Marchand £626,000, though all, of course, had big pots of share options – only worth anything if the company prospered. The latest bonuses were on a different scale.

"What imaginative remuneration consultants managed to construct a scheme the would ensure that the chief executive collected a bonus after presiding over the company's plunge deep into the red and a catastrophic share price performance?" asked Patience Wheatcroft, *The Times*' business editor.

"On Planet Reuters, life remains pretty sweet. Up there, the sun is always shining, buses run on time and money keeps rolling into directors' pockets, seemingly regardless of corporate performance."

"On Planet Reuters, life remains pretty sweet," said William Lewis in the *Sunday Times*. "Up there, the sun is always shining, buses run on time and money keeps rolling into directors' pockets, seemingly regardless of corporate performance."

Describing Glocer as "He Who Must Be Paid", Lewis went on: "For the little people on Planet Reuters, life it not very good at all," with nearly one in five due to lose their jobs. Should Glocer lose his, though, his contract would give him a pay-off of up to £2.2m plus share options.

In mid-March the shares closed in London at 95.5 pence, 94% below their peak just three years earlier. Reuters market value had dropped from £23bn to under £1.4bn, less than twice its value at flotation in 1984.

"We do not have any problems with world-class pay if we get world-class performance. The problem is world-class pay with village performance."

It wasn't just the press that carped. The National Association of Pension Funds and the Association of British Insurers, both representing major investors, called for the compensation packages to be scrapped. The NAPF went as far as to urge members to abstain from voting on Reuters remuneration report at its annual meeting. "We do not have any problems with world-class pay if we get world-class performance," it said. "The problem is world-class pay with village performance."

Hogg, a member of the remuneration committee, defended Glocer's package. But he, too, was under heavy fire after eighteen years as chairman. "There is a rising awareness," the *Financial Times* commented, "that the decline in the core information business, under pressure from rivals such as Bloomberg, dates back several years. Few believe that the man who chaired dozens of board meetings during this time can escape blame for what is widely seen as a long-standing culture of complacency towards the emerging threat."

Patience Wheatcroft echoed this sentiment. "Whatever the triumphs of his early years . . . it is clear that Sir Peter Job . . . did not leave the company best equipped to fight the likes of Bloomberg," she wrote. "The same judgment must also find Sir Christopher Hogg guilty. By staying too long, Sir Christopher has allowed a reputation as one of Britain's industrial heavy-hitters to be tarnished."

In the event, the shareholder revolt was a damp squib. Hogg, with his customary aplomb, steered the annual meeting comfortably through a wave of flak from individual share holders, many of them former Reuters journalists. The remuneration packages were overwhelmingly approved, in the face of a token revolt and a vote from the floor, by the institutional shareholders. The two big American institutional shareholders, both 'deep valley' opportunist investors, didn't even bother to turn up.

Hogg had previously chaired Courtaulds and Allied Domecq. One former Reuters colleague recalls Hogg had once dismissed talk of a crisis at Reuters, saying he had been through the same sort of thing at Courtaulds. "But Christopher," he reminded him, "Courtaulds no longer exists!"

He was now also chairman of pharmaceuticals giant Glaxo SmithKline where, just weeks after the Reuters annual meeting, shareholders voted against the company's pay policy, including a £15m 'golden parachute' for the chief executive, a protest unprecedented in British corporate history. Hogg was rapidly acquiring a reputation as Britain's principal proponent of fat-cattery.

A UK-government sponsored report on corporate governance had recently concluded that to chair two FTSE 100 companies was too great a responsibility for one individual. In an interview with *The Times* in April, Hogg said he had offered to step down when Job left, but the board asked him to stay on. Nevertheless, headhunters were now searching for his successor, he confirmed. He would go when the right person was found.

BACK TO BASICS

Nearly three years into his stewardship of Reuters, Glocer's much-vaunted project Gazelle had failed to deliver the promised shift to Internet delivery for Reuters product range, which was now being drastically slimmed down. 'Fast Forward', though, would continue and indeed accelerate this policy. The share price had picked up with the overall market recovery that followed the brief war in Iraq, but revenues were still predicted to drop another 12% in 2003 with no real recovery expected until 2006. By then, Reuters would have shed a third of its staff, more than 6,000 employees, and spent nearly £1bn restructuring.

Among those axed would be Philip Green, the most prominent casualty of the Fast Forward cutbacks. Once tipped as a possible future chief executive, he left Reuters at the end of June 2003 when his position of chief operating officer was abolished in what Glocer described as a move to simplify the senior management structure. In the wake of the remuneration row, Reuters made clear Green's severance package would be below the maximum £825,000 he was eligible to receive.

Reuters is pinning considerable hopes for the future on the platform of its former competitor Bridge, parts of which it acquired after it filed for bankruptcy in 2001, and Reuters Knowledge, a new Internet-based product launched in 2003. But Bloomberg has overtaken it and launched a fresh challenge with EBS in foreign exchange and Dealing, while lower-cost competitors still snipe away at the bottom end of the market.

Big questions remain unanswered. How will the company manage to migrate IDN onto the Bridge platform? Is the Bridge platform wholly Internet ready? Will Reuters finally be able to match its dream of downloading products, upgrades and invoices to a client via the public Internet? Can its core financial services products survive much longer the onslaught of melting markets, and competition from Bloomberg and cheap Internet competitors?

And will the price be to return Reuters to its roots – to being just a markets and news information provider? Does this spell the end of Reuters ambitions to be the all-in-one, one-stop market provider, the end of the technology dream that gathered pace under Job but found no direction? In seeking to become Jack-of-all-trades, had Reuters ended up being master of none?

Well, master of one, maybe. Glocer now talks about concentrating on Reuters as an information company – a far cry from the 'technology and connectivity' he heralded when first appointed. His decision to purchase Multex, a brokerage news service, is at least consistent with this strategy.

"What I'd rather do is deliver on being a great information company with important technology helpers, than not deliver on ten different ambitious strategies which never become real," he told an interviewer early in 2003.

At the same time, and although he has been judiciously astute at avoiding public criticism of his predecessor, he has come close to saying that he inherited a sick business.

"The hard truth is that the growth story has not been there

in the core business for some time, but that fact has been masked by the Internet bubble and a series of acquisitions," he told the *Financial Times* in October 2002.

Glocer sought to reassure the annual meeting in April 2003. The core business in 2002 had actually been profitable, after stripping out losses by subsidiaries and restructuring costs. But he outlined a 'slimline' Reuters for the future. The Fast Forward programme, he said, would "transform Reuters into a highly focused information company and streamline our complex product lines."

"We need to simplify our business and to truly understand the work flow of our clients," he added. He could have been reciting a sixteen-word summary of Bloomberg's market philosophy.

IVORY TOWERS

How different it had all looked just three years earlier. In truth, though, even before Glocer took over, the edifice behind the façade of that £23bn market valuation was already crumbling.

Monitor and Dealing had met specific market needs, if partly by accident. Rich and Instinet too had found ready markets but, in many other instances Reuters got carried away with technology, producing services embodying what its technicians and developers said could, or in some instances could not, be done, rather than responding to market needs. The culmination was the ruinously expensive Armstrong project and its malformed offspring, Reuters 3000, a horribly over-engineered, impossibly user-unfriendly failure.

"Did we mount a really effective response to Bloomberg?" asks Ure. "Not really, but we certainly tried. We are still trying."

Armstrong was the belated search for a 'Bloomberg-killer' that in the end failed to build databases or emulate Bloomberg's intuitive navigation and popular bolt-ons like messaging. Nobody had asked Reuters to 'kill' Bloomberg – there was never a compelling marketing argument to simply try to copy what a competitor had already achieved. In the view of many former senior executives, Monitor and Dealing had beguiled Reuters in believing in its own infallibility.

"I think that got built into the culture, that you'd got to do better than the market could conceive of," says Peter Sharrock, the former director of customer focus whose group Glocer closed down. "But actually I don't think that's a winning ticket forever. It's a thing that happens periodically. When the market then starts growing up and they're looking for how technology can be applied in their specialist niches, then the idea that you can beat everybody in the whole industry is not going to happen again. The way you survive in that kind of a market is to keep very close to the business."

Somehow, the decision makers, top management and marketing, failed to keep in touch with their markets, to the frustration of the sales staff and account managers.

"I don't think the marketing people actually ever met the users," Jonny Fitzgerald says. "They didn't know what the clients wanted. Marketing sat in ivory towers and had constant meetings, but never seemed to really get to know the customers. Their attitude was: 'We've given you this to sell, so you get out there and sell it, but don't ask us to come along'."

"They were nice enough guys, but you wouldn't have given them the remote control of the TV, let alone the finger on the control button of what Reuters was doing."

Top management became remote. "They were totally out of touch with what was happening on the ground," one former senior executive says. "Job gathered around him his favourites, who one by one let him down. They were nice enough guys, but you wouldn't have given them the remote control of the TV, let alone the finger on the control button of what Reuters was doing. They told Job what he wanted to hear, and if you sang another song, you weren't listened to."

"Leadership requires you to be prepared to live with people who are awkward, because it is from those people that you learn more than from those who say 'yes'," says Heinrich Wenzel. It was this growing remoteness that led to stagnation at the top of the company, and a growing aversion to risk, a loss of the entrepreneurial drive that had made Reuters successful.

"We certainly suffered from a lack of decisiveness on the part of a lot of managers who probably were promoted above their level of competence, and in a more cut-throat company probably wouldn't have survived," says one former executive committee member. "We built up a kind of civil service mentality, accountant mentality; everything had to go through enormous bureaucratic procedures, and it was only people who were sufficiently determined who could cut through them."

Few managed to do so, in particular to bring about the diversification needed to reduce over-dependence on the top tier of the financial markets.

"We clearly ended up still very dependent upon the financial services market which stumbled extremely badly over the last eighteen months," says Ure.

Reuters had, of course, diversified, but too often in a piecemeal and unstructured fashion, nickel and diming, too often choking off new initiatives before they could prosper and rarely spending more than $200m on acquisitions when what was perhaps needed was a $5bn strategic gambit. With its high share price and cash-generating business, this level of ambition was there for the taking. But instead the company gave more than £2bn back to shareholders.

Hogg, the former EXE member said, regarded this as "a very decisive management attitude, which it didn't seem to be to many of us."

Another former EXE member said Hogg and Job were concerned that major acquisitions might mean taking their eyes off ball. The problem was, he adds, "they ended up not acquiring anything but still taking their eyes off the ball."

Job, Ure, Villeneuve had worked alongside Renfrew, Long and Nelson when enormous risks were almost the norm, and had themselves not always been risk averse. "The fact is that these were the very people who'd stuck their necks way out over Monitor and Dealing, taking huge risks and taking the company into this whole electronic information age," one former top marketing executive says.

"If there's a lesson to be learned, it's that you need to dig over senior management every three or four years. When you've got guys who have been twenty, twenty-five years at the top of the company, it's very hard to keep the momentum going, to keep the innovation and the will to take risks."

In the final analysis, Job and his fellow board and executive committee members had no strategy, no clearly defined goals, no endgame in mind. After Monitor and Dealing, the only signs of strategy at Reuters were haphazard – seeing off Bloomberg, picking up acquisitions here, there and everywhere and then at first stumbling and latterly being dragged kicking and screaming into the Internet.

Reuters top management became reactive rather than pro-active. Job made a virtue of not having a strategy at the dawning of the Internet Age – precisely the time when strategy was called for. Reuters could have reinvented itself with the Internet and started over again on another flight path to rapid growth – if it had shed the heavy fixed costs it is now belatedly throwing over-board.

Many former executives feel high-level management expert-ise should have been brought in early in the 1990s as Reuters became a truly global giant. The Job–Ure–Villeneuve trium-virate "would have benefited from a serious challenge, and that challenge should have been initiated by the Chairman," one says. "What was needed was someone of real stature, an inter-national businessman who would have been at home in the upper echelons of an IBM or Microsoft," another adds.

Ure, though, denies there was bad blood between him and Job, describing them as 'best friends'. They are planning a golf-ing holiday, together with Marchand and Rowley, he adds. Not Parcell? "He doesn't play golf."

Had becoming a public company imposed too many dis-tractions, excessive focus on the share price and shareholder value? The rationale for going public is to allow companies to raise cash through the stock market to fund expansion, but Reuters generated so much cash that it never needed to do that. Did top executives become too preoccupied with the value of their share options, to the detriment of strategic thinking? The relative strength of the share price from late 1999 through to the early part of 2001 created a false sense that everything in the garden was rosy, when clearly it wasn't.

Might Reuters have been better off staying a private company? It didn't seem to have done Bloomberg any harm. But in reality, once the flotation ball was rolling it became an irresistible force; there was simply too much money at stake for the newspapers who owned Reuters.

Rupert Murdoch was at the centre of the flotation debate. "Doubtless, the concern over options, shareholder relations and all the rest was a real diversion," he told the authors. "But in itself, I do not think it was the prime cause of Reuters losing its market position. Leadership, both at the board and management levels, will have to take responsibility."

That lack of leadership perhaps became most apparent in the battle to succeed Job. As Marchand and Parcell fought it out for the chief executive's chair that neither was destined to get, the company was split down the middle. Isaac Piha, a senior vice-president at the time, says the vicious succession battle left Reuters 'rudderless'. Another former top manager agrees: "All of a sudden, the only people who could have worked together to respond to the challenges were at each other's throats because the succession was so badly handled."

TURNAROUND OR TAKEOVER?

Reuters is vulnerable to takeover. The Golden Share controlled by the trustees had always been flaunted as an effective barrier to a bid, but former non-executive director, Pehr Gyllenhammar, now chairman of the trustees, has made abundantly clear that this is not so. All that is required is that a bidder should be a company of status and repute, committed to maintaining Reuters editorial principles, and above all its editorial independence.

Reuters is vulnerable to takeover.

In the bear market of the past three years Reuters share price has underperformed both the FTSE-100 and media indices by around one-third. The share price has recovered a little in recent months but, if it remains low, the company will be vulnerable to a takeover. In a bull market, Reuters usually out-performs it rivals. But despite the post-Gulf War bounce, a bull market seems a long way off.

In reality, potential bidders are few. Speculation has centred on Thomson Corporation and Pearson. But Pearson currently seems to have enough problems of its own, without taking on Reuters as well, while Thomson is focused on an aggressive acquisition trail and expansion which it hopes will enable it to beat Reuters rather than buy it. It has hired several key ex-Reuters executives. Reed Elsevier, the giant Anglo-Dutch publishing group, has the muscle to buy and take on Reuters, but has looked closely in the past and shied away.

Another possible suitor might be McGraw-Hill, the US financial services, information, media and educational group. Its best-known brands include the Standard & Poor's credit rating service, which has been expanded to include investment analysis and research services, *BusinessWeek* magazine, Platt's energy information service and four US local TV stations. With a market capitalization of well over $10bn, it boasts healthy earnings and revenue growth – operating profits of over $1bn in 2002 on revenues of $4.8bn – and strong cash flow. Just a few years ago it might have been an ideal acquisition for Reuters.

Microsoft might be tempted by Reuters media content, and Murdoch's News Corporation could find synergies with its vast newspaper and television news interests. But why would they want the financial side of Reuters business?

Perhaps only for the brand – what Hogg calls the company's most valuable asset. Maybe it is the last really valuable asset and – if so – it belongs almost exclusively to the news agency. Revenues from Corporate and Media products were £315m in 2002 and, while not all this is attributable to Editorial's output, it takes no account of the value of the financial news. Editorial costs were only £216m, so even without putting a value on financial news services, Editorial appears to be an attractive proposition. Might a Microsoft or a News Corporation be tempted to keep the news services and sell off or close down the rest?

Perhaps Glocer's Fast Forward programme will run through to a successful conclusion at the end of 2005, when a leaner, meaner Reuters will be poised to take advantage of a sustained market upturn with a more focused product range, simplified, Internet-friendly delivery platforms and a lower cost base, able to see off its competitors and restore its former pre-eminence.

Many at Reuters believe Bloomberg is reaching its sell-by

date, becoming a sitting duck tied to twenty-year-old technology which Ure describes as 'antique' and making no apparent move to migrate to the Internet. "Who says he has won?" asks Ure.

Reuters also still dominates the very top end of the market with its all-singing, all-dancing 3000Xtra Version 4.5 providing the full range of real-time and historical data, analytics and a host of other applications. Glocer's slimline Reuters might also be well placed to prosper in a second dawning of the Internet Age, once the fallout from the bursting of the first dotcom bubble has settled. Reuters may have lost a few battles, but the war isn't over yet.

Indeed, chatting to one of the authors after April's annual meeting, Glocer said he looked forward to writing the preface to the second edition of this book, which he says will tell the story of how he turned the company around and restored its fortunes. That will be quite a book.

Authors' Note

We owe a debt of gratitude to many friends and former Reuters colleagues around the world who gave us their encouragement, their help and the benefit of their insights as we prepared this book. This project would not have been possible without them. They are too numerous to mention individually. Many are quoted in this book but others preferred anonymity, not because they lack conviction in their interpretation of the events described but because, like us and like almost every other former colleague we consulted, they share an abiding loyalty to Reuters.

We also all share a deep sadness at the speed and extent of Reuters decline from its position as the world's pre-eminent provider of news and financial information. This was a great and unique company, the ideals and standards of its news services, which underpinned every aspect of the enterprise, principles we could be proud to serve. Those we worked with, a glorious diversity of every race, religion and creed, were not just colleagues, they were family, sharing a common cause. Working for Reuters was not just a job; it was a way of life, and one we were privileged to enjoy.

We, and all those who have helped us, fervently hope it can be restored to its former pre-eminence, learn from the errors of its recent past.

Whether it can remains in doubt. In late July Reuters reported a return to a small profit in the first half of 2003, though this was achieved almost entirely through savage cost-cutting, with revenues continuing downward. Tom Glocer was cautiously optimistic but warned against forecasting too early a recovery. The same week, Interbrand, which puts a value on major international brands, said the Reuters brand had dropped by \$1.3bn in the past year to \$3.3bn – the steepest drop of any major international company – after a 12% drop the previous year.

Cost-cutting alone will not be enought to restore the value of the brand or Reuters overall fortunes. To achieve that, Reuters must claw back the market share it has lost to Bloomberg, which will mean launching new products that will win back customers and tap into new markets. Maybe – just maybe – the worst is past. But, as to whether a golden new dawn beckons, the distant horizon is still clouded.

Brian Mooney and Barry Simpson
August 2003

Reuters Timeline

1850   Paul Julius Reuter starts 'pigeon post' service between Brussels and Aachen

1851   Reuter moves to London

1858   Reuters begins supplying London newspapers

1865   Reuters Telegram Company registered in London. Two-hour news beat on assassination of President Abraham Lincoln. Alexandria office opened – the first outside Europe

1866   Atlantic cable connects Newfoundland–Ireland, Bombay offices opened, first in Asia

1871   Duke of Saxe-Coburg-Gotha confers baronetcy on Reuter

1878   Reuter retires, son Herbert takes over

1891   Baronetcy confirmed by Queen Victoria

1899   Reuter dies in Nice, aged 83, buried in London

1900   Two-day newsbeat on relief of Mafeking

1915   Herbert Reuter commits suicide, Roderick Jones becomes general manager

1920   Reuters Trade Department established to report financial news

1923   Continental Broadcasting Service carries prices and exchange rates to Europe in Morse

1925   PA takes majority shareholding

1928   City ticker service to banks started

1939   Reuters moves to 85 Fleet Street

1941   Reuters Trust established, Roderick Jones resigns, replaced by Christopher Chancellor. NPA members buy 50% of Reuters from PA

1945   Employees top 2,000

1947 AAP, NZPA become Reuters shareholders

1959 Walton 'Tony' Cole becomes general manager

1963 Gerald Long becomes General Manager

1964 Stockmaster launched

1967 Reuters starts independent reporting of US, ending deals with AP, Dow Jones

1970 Videomaster launched

1973 Reuters Monitor launched

1975 News Retrieval launched

1981 Dealing launched, Glen Renfrew becomes managing director, Michael Nelson general manager

1982 Bloomberg installs first terminals at Merrill Lynch

1984 Reuters becomes public company

1985 News pictures service launched, majority stakes in Visnews TV news agency and Rich Inc of Chicago acquired

1986 Acquisition of Instinet electronic share brokerage

1987 First IDN service, Equities 2000 launched. Triarch digital switching system for dealing rooms launched. Bloomberg opens first international offices, London and Tokyo

1988 Employees top 10,000

1989 Dealing 2000-1 launched, partnership agreement with Steve Levkoff's Capital Market Decisions

1990 Bloomberg launches news service

1991 Peter Job becomes managing director

1992 Dealing 2000-2, Globex, Treasury 2000 launched, full control of Visnews. Bloomberg Messaging launched

1993 Levkoff partnership terminated, Project Armstrong launched

1994 Teknekron and Quotron acquired, Reuters Financial TV launched, Bloomberg Television service starts

1995 Greenhouse Fund set up to invest in Internet ventures

1996 Reuters 3000 launched

1997 £1.5bn returned to shareholders. FBI starts undercover investigation of Reuters Analytics

1999 Factiva joint venture with Dow Jones. US Federal Grand Jury investigation of Reuters Analytics ends, no charges brought

2000   Dealing 3000 launched, Job says Reuters is an Internet company, Reuters share price tops record £17 on 7 March
2001   150th anniversary, Tom Glocer becomes managing director
2003   Glocer announced near £500m pre-tax loss for 2002 and 3,400 lay-offs. Reuters share price closes at 95.5p in London on 12 March. Bloomberg market share overtakes Reuters.

Glossary of Terms

AGM	annual general meeting
AOL	America On-Line, major US Internet service provider
AP	Associated Press, an American news agency
AFP	Agence France Presse, a French state-owned news agency
ART	Advanced Reuters Terminal, the first to run under Microsoft Windows
B2B	business to business
CEO	chief executive officer
CMD	Capital Markets Decisions, a Stamford-based company set up by Steve Levkoff
CNN	Cable News Network, US and world-wide TV news channel
DEC	Digital Equipment Corporation, major US computer equipment manufacturer
D&B	Dun & Bradstreet
EBS	foreign exchange dealing system launched by major banks in 1983 in competition with Reuters Dealing service
Effix	Paris-based software company acquired by Reuters
EMAP	British newspaper and magazine company
ESL	Sydney-based markets information, a technical analysis and graphics company acquired by Reuters
EXE	Reuters Executive Committee
FX	foreign exchange
forex	foreign exchange
FXFX	Reuters Monitor multicontributor Foreign Exchange page
GND	Reuters General News Division

GLOBEX after hours trading system for futures markets
GWR Major British commercial radio group
IDN Integrated Data Network, the 'pipe' that delivers Reuters data and news
IP Internet protocol
IPO initial public offering
ITN Independent Television News, a British TV news company
Instinet Electronic brokerage business acquired by Reuters in 1986
M&A mergers and acquisitions
MD managing director
MDC Market Data Corporation, company which markets Cantor Fitzgerald's data
NASDAQ National Association of Securities Dealers Automated Quotation – US 'over-the-counter' stock exchange, founded in 1971 as the world's first electronic stock market.
NCR US computer equipment manufacturer
NewMedia Reuters New Media business
NPA Newspaper Proprietors Association, grouping owners of British newspapers
OPEC Organization of Petroleum Exporting Countries
PA Press Association, the principal British domestic news agency
QRS Quotation Retrieval System, the forerunner of IDN
RAM Reuters North America
RA Reuters Asia
RES Reuters Economic Services
RT Reuters Terminal, a Windows-based Reuters screen
RTV Reuters Television (previously knows as Visnews)
SQL Structured Query Language, a computer language used to communicate with a database.
TRIARCH Trading Room Information Architecture, Reuters system for handling multiple vendor feeds.
TIBCO The software company spun out of Teknekron
UKI Reuters business division for United Kingdom and Ireland
UPI United Press International, an American News Agency
VAMP British provider of Healthcare information systems
VP vice-president

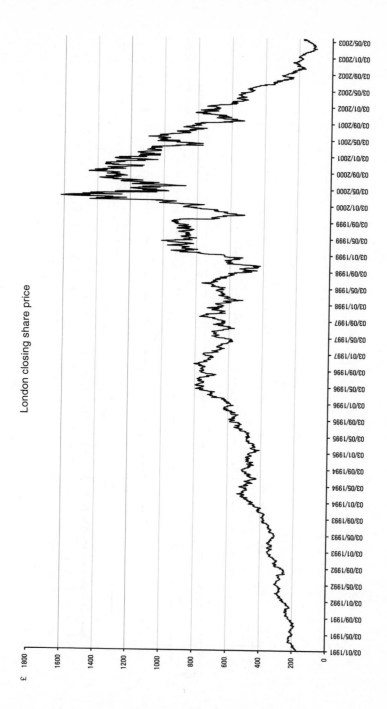

London closing share price

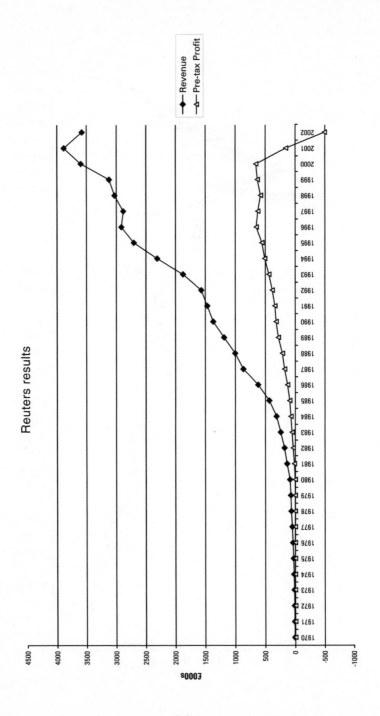

Reuters results

£000s

Index

217

Index